The
Real Food
Cookbook

By the Same Author

The Farmers' Market Cookbook

Real Food: What to Eat and Why

Real Food for Mother and Baby: The Fertility Diet, Eating for Two, and First Foods

The Real Food Cookbook

Traditional Dishes for Modern Cooks

Nina Planck

Photographs by Katherine Wolkoff

Enjoy real food!

Nina

BLOOMSBURY

NEW YORK · LONDON · NEW DELHI · SYDNEY

Published by Bloomsbury USA, New York

All papers used by Bloomsbury USA are natural, recyclable products made from
wood grown in well-managed forests. The manufacturing processes conform to the
environmental regulations of the country of origin.

LIBRARY OF CONGRESS CATALOGING-IN-PUBLICATION DATA HAS BEEN APPLIED FOR.

ISBN: 978-1-60819-675-3

First U.S. edition 2014

1 3 5 7 9 10 8 6 4 2

Designed and typeset by Jennifer S. Muller

Printed and bound in China by C&C Offset Printing Co. Ltd

contents

introduction

In my twenties, I found myself living in London, England, and sorely homesick for an inimitable and tactile experience of home. What I missed most was a weekly visit to a busy farmers' market, brimming with fresh, seasonal produce sold by the people who grew it. Most of all, I missed the food, but I also longed for the banal but quite pleasant background chatter of the small sale. "Yes, the beets are beautiful today . . . looks like it's just under two pounds . . . that'll be $7.50 . . . we'll have corn in two weeks . . . our chickens run free on grass . . . the red peppers are sweeter . . . Genovese is the best basil for pesto . . . let the melon ripen on the counter till tomorrow . . . the garlic scape pesto was delicious, thank you . . . see you next Saturday." This was the agreeable if repetitive city soundtrack back when my rural Virginia family sold homegrown produce and flowers at Washington, D.C., farmers' markets.

As a girl, I had no idea that my parents were farming legends and market pioneers. Nor did they. I knew only that we were farmers and that every single dollar we earned, some person at some farmers' market had handed to us in exchange for fresh vegetables, berries, herbs, flowers, or eggs. Long mornings spent standing barefoot on the blacktop at the farmers' market marked me with a lifelong habit.

When I left the farm at eighteen years old, I found that life without a good market was dry, tasteless. And in the capital of Cool Britannia in 1999, there was no such thing.

Of course there were markets in London, some of them ancient. But they weren't selling what I needed. The street markets sold Dutch tomatoes along with batteries, dustpans, and tube socks, and in the smaller organic shops and markets, the superior attitude, rubbery carrots, and high prices turned me off. My fantasy was to ship an entire market load from my parents' Wheatland Vegetable Farms—two trucks of gorgeous, ecological vegetables destined for one of our best markets, Takoma Park in Maryland—on the Concorde. I would set up our stand, just like at home, next to the shabby imported produce. The fabulous display of fine vegetables would cause a riot and change the world.

Eventually I hit on the simpler idea of asking local farmers to bring their produce to London, and to my delight, a dozen farmers agreed. On June 6, 1999, I opened my first farmers' market—and London's first modern farmers' market—in Islington, not far from my house. All I wished for was a place to buy fresh peas, strawberries, and apples from local farms. I knew that Londoners would love food straight from the farm, too—but I didn't realize how much. The markets were a sensation. In three months I opened two more. Today we organize about two dozen year-round markets. In a few short years, farmers' markets in England, Scotland, and Wales blossomed. My fantasy had come true.

Yet the markets also proved humbling. It was soon clear that I knew very little about much of the food our farmers were selling. In those days, I still suffered under the impression that a low-fat, vegetarian diet, with perhaps a bit of fish, was the only healthy one. Meanwhile, alongside the lovely produce I'd longed for, the fine farmers at London Farmers' Markets were selling foods seldom seen at an American farmers' market back then. Right from the start, we had grass-fed beef, heritage pork, fat Christmas goose, wild venison, raw-milk cheeses, high-fat butter, and thick cream. It did not escape my notice that these fine ingredients brought rosy cheeks and a great deal of pleasure to our loyal customers.

It was time for me to eat these traditional foods and (more intimidating) to learn to cook them. So I did, with happy results. My health was never better and my meals never more delicious. Soon I was gathering the research to support the case for traditional foods in *Real Food: What to Eat and Why*. But the path from a limited, anxiety-driven diet to conscientious omnivory and polymorphous delight in food—as a cook and an eater—was long, and I made many mistakes. With this book, perhaps I can spare you a few wrong turns. For this is the cookbook I needed when I learned that traditional foods from land, sea, and sky are not only tasty but also good for you.

It's an idiosyncratic collection. The recipes here are those of a farmers' daughter, former vegetarian, and home cook. They reflect the rhythms of my life with a cheesemonger husband and three small children. The ingredients are timeless, not trendy; the methods classic rather than rule-breaking. Above all, these are the dishes I love, made with real food.

drinks & nibbles

Kombucha ÷ Raw-Milk Kefir ÷ Water Kefir

Fermented Ginger Ale ÷ Fermented Watermelon Basil Cooler

Blueberry Soda ÷ Chocolate Egg Cream ÷ Cucumber Lemonade

The Greenery: A Cucumber Gin Cocktail

Drinking Chocolates ÷ Hot Chocolate ÷ Hot Cocoa

Fried Cheese Curds ÷ Jalapeño Poppers

Brined & Roasted Nuts

drinks

My brother and I were raised by a water purist. My mother drinks water and water only. She might flirt with a glass of raw milk, and she indulges in coffee as often as she swears off it, but I suspect no commercial soft drink has ever passed her lips. Sweaty noonday farmhands must drink, however, so we carried jugs of well water in the green flatbed Ford on scratchy mulch runs all over Loudoun County, and we left water jugs in the shade while hoeing pumpkins far from the house. In those long, dusty pumpkin rows, I often fantasized about the real lemonade Laura and Mary Ingalls carried to Pa and the farmhands who were bringing in the hay. On family car trips in dead of winter, our feet dangled over half-frozen water jugs. There I'd be, thirsty on the Pennsylvania turnpike in twenty-degree February. Holding the heavy, frozen bottom of the milk jug, I tipped the just-melting ice water over my shivering gums. I still hate ice cubes.

When we were little, my mother used to buy frozen orange juice in cardboard tubes—slicing the granular cylinder with a butter knife in the bottom of a worn blue plastic pitcher—but I can only assume that this was a concession to the presence of children in the house, because I have no memory of her drinking juice of any kind. And today my mother makes the same innocent, politely surprised expression when she is invited to "meet for a drink" or encounters a commercial drink, as if she could not quite fathom that one would pay to quench thirst. Soda, it goes without saying, is the work of the devil.

But things have changed, and now there are soft drinks that might tempt even Susan Planck. A few years ago, my parents—pioneers in modern ecological farming and farmers' markets—finally quit farming after nearly forty seasons. Today they are not merely retired but also justifiably eminent, and they dwell in the center of a large social circle that consists of many young and lively farmers. Unlike my mother, these farmers are habitual drinkers of all manner of traditional beverages, from wine, beer, and spirits to softer stuff, such as kvass, kefir, and kombucha. All these drinks are fermented or cultured in some fashion, which suits the generation of ecological land-workers whose farms are sprouting on the very land where I grew up. In addition to honing their banjo and whittling skills, many farmers I know nurture billion-strong living bacterial communities in their kitchens. They tend these microbiomes as carefully as they tend the finely calibrated compost that is the foundation of their farming habits. These food makers explicitly connect the internal, personal biome in your gut, which is fed by the enzymes and probiotics in these homebrews, and the equally vital biome in the topsoil, which feeds the plants we eat and the pasture the animals nibble and graze. Before I had children, I used to visit my parents and play guest cook while they loaded market trucks. In those days, I'd open a bottle of wine from the vineyard next door while I went about gathering and chopping up vegetables. When I visit my beloved Wheatland, Virginia, today, I raise a kombucha cocktail to a new generation of tangy, fizzy, and healthy drinks—and to the farmers and brewers who make them.

kombucha

Makes 2½ quarts

Kombucha is a nonalcoholic fermented tea originally from Northeast China or Manchuria. From there it spread to Russia and beyond. I used to drink it purely for health, not pleasure; it suits my digestion and cures my gloom. But to my surprise, our children like it—Rose, at one and a half, called it her "cocktail"—and I like it too. Home-brewed kombucha is cheaper than store-bought and typically less fizzy. Alas my brewing habits are modest. My chef friend Emily Duff, however, has a fridge brimming with living drinks, so I asked her to write recipes for kombucha, kefir, and other grown-up soft drinks made with real flavors and real sugar.

To make the first batch, you'll need a little store-bought kombucha and a SCOBY, which stands for Symbiotic Culture of Bacteria and Yeast. The SCOBY, which also kick-starts fermented foods such as ginger beer and sourdough bread, is best found on the real food underground. A moist, mushroom-like living colony resembling a pancake, it devours the caffeine in the tea and the sugar, creating the good things in kombucha: B vitamins, enzymes, and antioxidant glucaronic acid. In Chinese, it's called kouba, or "yeast mother." The mother will make a few batches of kombucha, yielding a "baby" each time, until it wears out. To start your first batch, ask a friend for a fresh baby—and then give your own babies away. (The fermented food world is keen on these timeless household transfers.) You'll need a one-gallon glass jar or a large glass bowl and smaller glass soda bottles with tight lids.

3 qts water
1 c organic whole cane sugar
4 black or green organic tea bags
8 oz raw organic kombucha
1 SCOBY

1. Boil the water.
2. Add the sugar and dissolve for about 5 minutes.
3. Add the tea bags, turn off the flame, and cover. Let it cool.
4. When the liquid is at room temperature, remove the tea bags and transfer it to a 1-gallon glass jar or bowl.
5. Add the kombucha to the cool sweetened tea.
6. Place the SCOBY on top of the tea. Crisscross the lid with masking tape and date it. Cover it with a tea towel and move it somewhere neither hot nor cold.
7. In 5 days, taste it. The kombucha should have lost its sweetness and tea flavor and be slightly tart with a fizz.
8. Leave it for 7 to 10 days until it tastes the way you like it.
9. Pour it into glass soda bottles, seal, and refrigerate. A second fermentation, which yields more nutrients, flavor, and fizz, occurs in the smaller bottles. Drink it within 2 weeks. ✛

Flavored Kombucha

When you pour the kombucha into bottles for the second fermentation,
add a flavor. The berry, ginger, and lemon flavors are great together.

Berry

Add ¼ cup of finely chopped frozen raspberries, blueberries, strawberries,
or other berries to the bottle and seal. Leave out for 3 to 5 days and then refrigerate.

Ginger

Add 1 tablespoon of freshly grated ginger and its juice and ¼ teaspoon of organic whole
cane sugar to the bottle and seal. Leave out for 3 to 5 days and then refrigerate.

Pomegranate

Add 1 tablespoon of organic pomegranate (or any fruit) syrup to the
bottle and seal. Leave out for 3 to 5 days and then refrigerate.

Lemon

Add 3 tablespoons of fresh Meyer lemon juice and ¼ teaspoon of organic
whole cane sugar and seal. Leave out for 3 to 5 days and then refrigerate.

Kombucha Cocktails

Ginger Bubbles

Mix equal parts Ginger Kombucha and chilled Champagne in a glass and give it a twist of lemon.

Ginberry Cooler

Pour 1½ ounces of gin over ice. Fill the glass with Berry Kombucha and give it a twist of lime or lemon.

raw-milk kefir

Makes 2 quarts

Kefir—from the Turkish for "foam"—is a fermented milk with origins in the North Caucasus region, where shepherds likely discovered that fresh milk carried in leather pouches would sometimes turn into a tasty carbonated drink. Traditional kefir was made in skin bags and then hung near a doorway, where the bag would be knocked by passersby, ensuring regular, gentle mixing. Like kombucha, it is now made all over the world. You will make it by inoculating cow, goat, or sheep milk with kefir grains, which you can buy online from Cultures for Health or borrow from a kefir maker—and which will grow in size and multiply with each batch you make. As with yogurt, the lactose (or milk sugar) in kefir is largely broken down, making it easy to digest. Drink kefir for its enzymes, probiotics, and vitamins (B1, B12, and K2). For a bigger nutritional kick, make it with unpasteurized milk, which pairs the buzzing enzyme life of untreated milk with the probiotic oomph of the kefir. Emily Duff suggests you play with flavor combinations in the first brewing by adding ginger, lemongrass, vanilla bean, dried cherries, mango, cardamom, star anise, cloves, or fresh herbs. A store-bought kefir starter yields three or four batches. The homegrown kefir grains that come from a batch of milk kefir live forever.

2 T kefir grains
3 c raw milk

1. Put the kefir grains and milk in a 2-quart glass jar and cover loosely with the lid.
2. Place it on a shelf at room temperature for 1 to 2 days. Gently turn the jar every few hours to disturb the liquid and inspire the grains to grow.
3. The kefir is ready when it resembles yogurt in texture and consistency and has a pleasant, tangy flavor with a little fizz. Move the jar. If bubbles fly up from the bottom and it has a sour bite, it is ready.
4. Strain the liquid through a cloth or sieve, bottle it, and refrigerate. Drink it within 2 weeks.
5. Reserve the kefir, which keeps much longer: fermentation, yielding more bubbles and a more pronounced sour taste, will continue. Put the kefir grains in a glass jar, top them with raw milk, and keep them in the fridge for the next batch. ✢

water kefir

Makes 2 quarts

Water kefir makes a fine probiotic for those who avoid dairy.

8-10 unsulfured dried apricots
1 Meyer lemon
1 qt water
½ c organic whole cane sugar
⅓ c kefir grains

1. Chop the apricots.
2. Cut the lemon in half, slice one half, and save the other for something else.
3. In a bowl, dissolve the sugar in water. Add the kefir grains, apricots, and lemon slices.
4. Transfer to a 2-quart glass jar and seal. Leave it at room temperature for 3 days.
5. Strain the liquid and transfer it to smaller airtight soda bottles and leave out for another 24 hours. It's ready to drink. Refrigerate and drink within 2 weeks. ✢

fermented ginger ale

Makes 2 quarts (about 8 drinks)

In the late nineteenth and early twentieth century, ginger ale was said to be the most popular soft drink in America. Ginger itself is a zingy tonic. Here, the whey works the fermentation magic, producing the probiotics (which serve your digestion), the flavor (which is tangy), and the fizz (which is merely fun).

Use fresh whey, not powdered. If you can't find it, make your own. Just strain a quart of yogurt through a fine cloth for most of the day. You'll have lovely thick yogurt and a pint of whey, which keeps for weeks in the fridge and can be used for all sorts of projects, like tzatziki.

1 large knob of fresh ginger
4 Meyer lemons
4-6 limes, depending on size
¼ c orange blossom honey
½ tsp unrefined sea salt
2 T fresh whey
6 c water

1. Wash, but do not peel, the ginger. Grate the ginger on the finest grater you have to yield about 2 tablespoons.
2. Squeeze the lemons and limes to yield ¼ cup of each juice.
3. Combine all the ingredients in a 2-quart glass bottle. Mix thoroughly and seal.
4. Leave it at room temperature for 3 to 7 days, letting air pressure out periodically so as to avoid building up too much carbon dioxide.
5. Refrigerate and drink within 2 weeks. ✢

fermented watermelon basil cooler

Makes 2 quarts

The tasty watermelon of my youth was a green-and-white-striped Crimson Sweet, about the size of a basketball, weighing 10 to 20 pounds. It was an All-America Selection Winner in 1964, and it's still one of the sweetest open-pollinated heirloom varieties that farmers grow. A little one called Yellow Doll isn't bad either.

8–10 lb watermelon
8–10 Meyer lemons
small bunch of Genovese basil
¼ c organic whole cane sugar
¼ c fresh whey
1 T unrefined sea salt
3 c water

1. Make 3 cups of watermelon juice in a blender or food processor. Don't strain the pulp.
2. Squeeze 1 cup of lemon juice.
3. Take ½ cup of basil leaves and gently bruise them using a mortar and pestle to release the oil.
4. Put all the ingredients in a 2-quart glass jar, cover with water, and close the lid tightly.
5. Stir and leave out at room temperature for 3 days. Allow a little carbonation to escape when necessary and replace the cap firmly. Chill and serve. Keeps up to 2 weeks in the fridge. ✢

Watermelon Basil Fermentini

Pour 1 ounce of vodka over ice, add 6 ounces of Watermelon Basil Cooler, and shake vigorously. Garnish with watermelon and basil.

blueberry soda

Makes 2 cups (32 tablespoons) of syrup, enough for sixteen 8-ounce sodas with 2 tablespoons each

Here's a zippy soft drink you can make year-round if you jar or freeze the syrup, which is also delicious on pancakes and ice cream.

1 lime
4 c blueberries
1 c water
2 T organic whole cane sugar
6 oz sparkling water for each drink

1. Zest and juice the lime, setting the juice aside.
2. In a saucepan, bring the berries, lime zest, and water to a boil.
3. Simmer for 10 minutes, then strain through cheesecloth to remove any particles.
4. Return the liquid to the pan. Add the sugar and lime juice and cook until the sugar is dissolved, about 5 minutes. Cool and refrigerate for up to 2 weeks.
5. To serve, put two tablespoons of blueberry syrup and six ounces of sparkling water in a glass and stir. ✢

chocolate egg cream

Makes 1½ cups (24 tablespoons) of syrup, enough for eight 10-ounce egg creams

Don't look for eggs or cream in this famous New York soda fountain drink. An egg cream is a fizzy soda made with milk and flavored, typically, with vanilla or chocolate syrup. It's usually associated with Brooklyn, home of its alleged inventor, candy store owner Louis Auster. Do use a seltzer with sturdy bubbles, such as Canada Dry or Gerolsteiner, an old-fashioned German mineral water so feisty it tastes like a quarry. Or you can add fizz to your own tap water with a store-bought hand pump, as we do at our country place. Emily Duff sometimes makes her egg creams with raw-milk kefir in place of milk, which makes an exquisite tangy real soda. You can easily add a subtle fruitiness with reduced tart cherry juice, a delicious, tangy, and antioxidant-rich syrup that I buy online from Michigan orchards. (We also make "cocktails" for children with cherry syrup. Just drop a splash of cherry syrup in the bottom of a glass and fill it with kombucha, fresh juice, or sparkling water.

My instructions are explicit, because I've closely watched Emily make this drink. The large glass, the long spoon, and the repeated "whipping up" are all necessary.

For one 10-ounce chocolate egg cream
3 T chocolate syrup
¼ c cold milk (or about 1 inch in the glass)
6 oz seltzer (or enough to fill the glass)
½–1 tsp tart cherry juice syrup (optional)

The syrup must be warm enough to pour easily. Let it come to room temperature if the day is warm, or heat it very gently.
1. Pour an inch of cold milk in a tall (10-ounce) glass. Whip it up vigorously with a long-handled teaspoon until there is a little head of foam.
2. Add a splash of the seltzer, leaving at least an inch at the top of the glass. Again, whip it up from the bottom until there is a good head of foam.
3. Dribble the chocolate syrup and the (optional) tart cherry juice syrup into the milk. Again, whip it up from the bottom until the milk is dark brown and the top is thick with foam. Drink at once. ✛

For the Chocolate Syrup
Use a high-quality cocoa powder, such as Pernigotti. (see "The Pantry," page 235). This chocolate syrup also makes a fine topping for vanilla ice cream.

¾ c cocoa powder
1 c organic whole cane sugar
⅛ tsp unrefined sea salt
½ c water
1 tsp vanilla extract

1. Mix the dry ingredients well. Mix those with the water and vanilla in a small saucepan. Whisk over low heat until the ingredients are lump-free and fully blended, 5 minutes or less. You are *blending,* not cooking, the chocolate.
2. Cool at room temperature. Refrigerate for up to 2 weeks. ✛

cucumber lemonade

makes 12 small (4-ounce) or 6 large (8-ounce) drinks

When I was little, we grew two kinds of cucumbers: regulars and picklers. The regulars were dark green, with thick skin and modest flavor; you still see these unfortunate vegetables at farm stands. The picklers were small, thin-skinned, and flecked with white. We ate the picklers. In their later farming days, my parents dropped the regulars and grew many tasty cukes. The better picklers, picked when they are slightly triangular rather than puffed out, still taste wonderful, as do the long, curvy Asian types and the now-popular Persian (sometimes called Lebanese) varieties, which are small, smooth, and round on both ends. The variety that started the Persian craze was Beit Alpha, named for a Byzantine-era synagogue of the same name in northern Israel. These cosmopolitan cukes were developed from English, Dutch, Japanese, Chinese, and Indian varieties on a neighboring kibbutz. Bitterness, by the way, is usually a function of dry weather and overmature cucumbers. Commanding the weather is not in your gift, but do look for younger cukes.

Farmers please note: the flavor of overirrigated cucumbers is diluted and bland. Cooks: if you can't tell a good cucumber by eye, ask your farmer for samples to taste.

8 Meyer lemons
1 large thin-skinned cucumber or 2 small ones
1 knob of fresh ginger
handful of mint
6 c water, still or sparkling
2-3 T organic whole cane sugar, or to taste

1. Zest 1 lemon.
2. Squeeze the remaining lemons to yield about 1 cup of juice.
3. Peel the cucumber and slice it very thin on a mandolin or grater, to yield about ¼ cup.
4. Wash, but do not peel, the ginger and grate it finely to yield about 1 tablespoon.
5. Crush the mint leaves.
6. Put all the ingredients except the water in a pitcher. Add the water, stir, pour it over ice, and serve. ✢

the greenery: a cucumber gin cocktail

Makes 1 cocktail

I was at least ten years late to the cocktail trend, but now that the better barkeeps have gone locavore, I've been tempted by organic American-grain vodkas, like Crop, and small-batch gins, like Rob's Mtn Gin, brewed in Boulder, Colorado, with local juniper and other botanicals. But for me, the seduction of the cocktail derives from the plants: my favorite food group. Cucumber, watermelon, sour cherry, rosemary, lemon, butternut squash, serrano chili, thyme—the modern drinks menu reads like a seed catalog. It's also coming to resemble the apothecary of a wild-crafting herbalist: spirit-makers and bartenders use wild mint, pinesap, mugwort, and sassafras. For one hot summer party, we spread out the elements of a make-your-own Cobb salad and I created "The Greenery," a summer gin cocktail. Stephany Munera, a lovely Colombian architecture student who was then taking care of our children, offered to tend bar. We fiddled with the drink until it was perfect. Then I spotted Stephany, still tinkering. Her final touch was a grind of sea salt right on top of the ice. This drink is dry—only the St-Germain, a liqueur made with fresh Alpine elderflowers—gives it a little sweetness. How much is a "splash"? The technical answer seems to be one-eighth of an ounce, or just under a teaspoon, but when I asked the professionals, the answers were more poetic: "A short beat." "Two dribbles." Our splash is a generous tablespoon. These proportions make one drink. It's easy to make more, but you'll have to eyeball the cucumber quantity: a dozen tender Persian types make about one quart of juice. This is also a stiff drink; if you reduce the alcohol, cut the gin and not the St-Germain. Otherwise, it is very austere.

2 cucumbers
1 lime
1–3 lemon verbena leaves
1–3 spearmint leaves
1 T St-Germain
2 oz (4 T) gin
club soda (bubbles and bicarbonate of soda), seltzer (firm bubbles), or sparkling water (soft ones)
grind of unrefined sea salt

1. Peel and juice a cucumber. (I don't have a juicer, so I put the cucumber in the blender and squeeze the juice through a fine cloth for a fine, clear juice. Not strictly necessary, but nice.) You can do this one day ahead. Cover and refrigerate the juice.
2. When you are ready to mix the drink, slice the remaining cucumber. Put two slices of cucumber, 2 teaspoons of cucumber juice, a slice of lime, a leaf or two of lemon verbena and spearmint, and a splash of St-Germain in a large glass or shaker. Muddle it.
3. Add the gin and as many ice cubes as will fit in your glass or shaker. Shake it.
4. Pour the drink into the serving glass and fill with club soda, seltzer, or sparkling water.
5. Top with another ice cube if it'll fit. Grind sea salt right on top.
6. Garnish with a slice of cucumber or lime or a leaf of lemon verbena or spearmint. ✢

drinking chocolates

We make everyday chocolate milk with the finest cocoa powder and fresh whole milk—or raw milk when we have it. Pernigotti, the cocoa powder I prefer, is so good that we drink chocolate milk unsweetened (hot and cold) year-round. I use one to two tablespoons of chocolate powder, which is very dark, per cup and let the children thin that to taste with fresh milk. We often add a pinch of cinnamon, and sometimes a dead-ripe banana, to the blender. When I don't want to share mine, I add cayenne. Because the vast majority of our chocolate drinks are unsweetened, it's a real treat when we add any sugar. For sweetened cold chocolate milk, add two tablespoons of Chocolate Syrup (page 12) to each eight-ounce glass and mix well.

hot chocolate

Makes 4 cups; for one mug, the proportions are 25 grams of chocolate
(or ¼ bar) and 1 cup of milk

Even good hot cocoa is a pauper's drink compared with the luxury of hot chocolate. Drink them side by side, and you will immediately taste the silky difference. Happily, it takes no time at all to melt a chocolate bar. Most good chocolate bars (of any percentage cocoa) contain one hundred grams, or three and a half ounces, so that's how I measure chocolate for drinks, baking, and all other purposes. For Mexican hot chocolate, add the cinnamon and cayenne to the pan as you whisk in the milk.

1 bar (100 g or 3.5 oz) 70% chocolate
4 c milk, plus 1 c for serving
grind of unrefined sea salt
pinch of cinnamon (optional)
pinch of cayenne (optional)
whipped cream (optional)
1 nutmeg (optional)

1. Break up the chocolate bar. In a pan over a water bath, melt the chocolate, stirring constantly. Do not *cook* the chocolate; *melt* it.
2. Add a small amount of milk to make a thick paste. Don't rush this part. When the paste is completely smooth, add the rest of the 4 cups of milk and the salt, and whisk it well.
3. Add the optional cinnamon and cayenne.
4. Ladle it into mugs and serve piping hot with the extra cup of milk. Top with whipped cream and grated nutmeg. ✢

hot cocoa

Makes 4 cups; for one mug, the proportions are 1 cup of milk,
2 tablespoons of cocoa, 1 teaspoon of sugar, and extra milk or whipped cream to taste

The difference between hot cocoa and hot chocolate is cocoa butter. Cocoa is made with milk and cocoa powder. (Do not consider making cocoa with water; it's too thin, and nothing complements the flavor of chocolate like the flavor of milk.) Hot chocolate is made with milk and melted chocolate; the cocoa butter makes it velvety. You *could* make cocoa with cream, which contains more butterfat than milk, but the fat tends to float in droplets. The key to superior cocoa is superior cocoa powder, such as Pernigotti, which has 20 percent fat (more than most) and a rich, smooth flavor. This is my idea of a perfectly sweetened cup of cocoa. You can mix all the milk with the chocolate at once, but I prefer to make a batch that is quite dark, and then give the children fresh milk (hot or cold) so that each one can thin or cool his mug *his* way. Mixing one's own drink is a pleasure not soon outgrown.

4 c milk, plus 1 c for serving
8 T cocoa powder
4 tsp organic whole cane sugar (or less)
grind of unrefined sea salt
pinch of cinnamon (optional)
⅛ tsp vanilla (optional)
pinch of cayenne (optional)
whipped cream (optional)

1. Put 4 cups of milk in a blender or food processor. Add the cocoa powder, sugar, salt, and (optional) cayenne, cinnamon, and vanilla. Blend until it's very smooth. (You can first make a milk-cocoa paste by hand, but cocoa binds easily and removing the lumps requires patience, which evades me. The machine works perfectly every time, and it foams nicely.)
2. Pour the chocolate milk into a pan. Over very low heat—or over a water bath—warm it, stirring or whisking constantly, until the smell of alcohol in the vanilla disappears.
3. Ladle it into mugs and serve piping hot with the remaining cup of milk. Or whipped cream. Or both. ✛

nibbles

When Rob and I were first going out (or more precisely, staying in), he often came over for dinner. One fall night I put out some sliced turnips and apples, a combination of crunch, sweetness, and spice, while I finished making dinner in my tiny kitchen. "Is this your idea of an appetizer?" Rob called. I squirmed with embarrassment and stiffened with pride. "Well, yes," I said. "My mother always set out raw vegetables before dinner. What is your idea of an appetizer?" His list involved pigs in blankets, Swedish meatballs, and tiny lamb chops. I assumed he was kidding. All I could picture was steam table food at a lousy wedding. Plus, they were foods I'd never eat before dinner. Lamb? Appetite-killer. Rob, for his part, thought my little plate of crudités was good for farm animals. I don't remember a moment when we were so deeply—and mutually—offended. He married me, but my appetizer skills have not improved. If it's a party, we'll set out cheese. If it's summer, I'll have bowls of cherry tomatoes around. These three nibbles also suit my simple tastes.

fried cheese curds

Serves 2

Children of cheesemakers in Ellsworth, Wisconsin—
and in any traditional cheddar country, such as
England and Ireland—know the characteristic
squeak of day-old cheese curds. They're like fresh
Roma tomatoes to a saucemaker: the ever-bountiful,
always-available raw ingredient. Curds are the
acorn-sized, raggedy balls of curdled milk before
it's chopped in small bits, cooked, and stacked—or
"cheddared." Curds taste of fresh milk. Biochemists
of taste have identified our sixth and seventh tastes—
for fat and for calcium—but they're struggling to
make the latter as famous as *umami*, our fifth taste,
the taste for protein. Because there is no catchy word
for what calcium tastes like, I nominate "cheese
curdy." You'll see breaded and deep-fried curds at
county fairs, but I leave deep-frying to the experts
and settle for a small pile of hot, gooey cheese
with a brown skin. My son Jacob loves them.

6 oz Ellsworth Cooperative Creamery cheese curds
flour for dusting
pinch of cayenne (optional)
a little unsalted butter or olive oil
freshly ground black pepper (optional)
minced parsley (optional)

1. Dust the curds with flour and perhaps a pinch of
cayenne.
2. Heat a thin slick of butter or olive oil in a frying pan—no
more than that, or there will be too much fat once the cheese
begins to release its butterfat—until it's hot but not smoking.
3. Put the curds in the pan in one layer and brown on one side
for about 30 seconds. Flip them and brown the other side.
4. Eat at once, topped with the black pepper and parsley if
you like. ✦

jalapeño poppers

These are great on a hot day and great with a beer. You'll pack a tablespoon or two of cheese in each pepper.

10 green jalapeño peppers
½ lb white or yellow cheddar

1. Set the oven to 350°F.
2. Cut the peppers in half lengthwise and scrape out the seeds. Leave the stems on.
3. Grate the cheese on the largest hole of the grater.
4. Pack the peppers with cheese.
5. Place them in a cast-iron skillet and bake until the peppers are mostly soft and the cheese is bubbling, 10 to 15 minutes. ✢

brined & roasted nuts

Raw and roasted nuts are as different as bread and toast. I love raw nuts of all kinds, but brining and toasting adds flavor and crunch. Unlike airline nuts, these don't need hydrogenated vegetable oil, dextrose, and artificial flavorings. They do benefit from real salt. Soaking is a form of mild fermentation, which helps to remove phytic acid, an anti-nutrient found in most grains and seeds. Phytic acid is a mild toxin meant to keep predators away. Squirrels get around this by burying acorns, which then ferment mildly, reducing the toxicity. (Soybeans, by the way, contain the most toxic phytic acids of all seeds. That's why traditional, fermented soy foods, such as miso, are nutritionally superior to plain soy protein.) A soak in saltwater also suffuses the whole nut with salt, not merely the surface. Roast nuts at a low temperature—the lower and slower the better—to protect the valuable omega-3 oils, which are damaged by high temperature. Do experiment with how dark you let them get; I prefer them blond. A dehydrator (which I don't own) is probably better than the oven. Now that my father makes his walnuts with an electric vegetable dryer, they are more evenly browned than the nuts from his oven or mine. Brined and roasted walnuts are delicious with roasted beets or in green salads with ripe pear and blue cheese. Pecans soak up the salt beautifully and become even more buttery with toasting; they're perfect on the cheese board. Toasted pumpkin seeds are wonderful on salads with thinly sliced fennel and a dressing of strong olive oil and fresh orange juice. Almonds I toast without soaking, since the brine seems to make them chewy, not crispy, and the salt doesn't sink in. Just sprinkle almonds with salt and water (to help the salt stick) and roast them in a low oven.

2 c walnuts, pecans, hazelnuts, or pumpkin seeds
2 T unrefined sea salt, plus extra for sprinkling

1. Put the nuts or seeds in a glass bowl and cover with water. Stir in the salt. The exact amount of salt is not important.
2. Let the nuts or seeds soak at room temperature for at least 6 hours or overnight.
3. Set the oven to 200°F. (You can use a lower temperature; just add time.)
4. Drain and quickly rinse the nuts or seeds. Spread them in one layer on a pan and grind a little more salt over them while they are still moist. The salt on the outside is merely tasty.
5. Roast them until crispy, about 2 or 3 hours. Once they cool, store them in jars or tins for up to a month. ✢

salads

Zucchini Carpaccio ⊹ Cuban House Salad

Iceberg and Tomatoes with Blue Cheese Dressing

Cobb Salad ⊹ Egg Salad ⊹ Deviled Eggs ⊹ Cobb Salad Deviled Eggs

Sauce Gribiche ⊹ Shaved Fennel, Apple, and Radish Salad

Caesar Salad ⊹ Mediterranean Salad

Tomatoes and Burrata ⊹ German Potato Salad

Green Salad with Walnuts, Blue Cheese, and Champagne Dressing

Tongue Salad

zucchini carpaccio

Serves 4

Apart from sliced tomatoes and salad leaves, it isn't easy to interest me in raw vegetables. Most I prefer cooked to perfection. This recipe is pretty, it's easy, and because the ribbons of zucchini are delicate and tender, it tempts even skeptics of crunch. Buy yellow and green zucchini, preferably young and small ones with thin skins and underdeveloped seeds. I prefer the ribbons broad and bite-sized—about three inches long—but they can also be long and skinny. Dress this salad at the very last minute, just before you serve it; otherwise the olive oil drenches the thin ribbons. I send heartfelt thanks to my friend Robin Shuster, a fine home cook and fellow farmers' market entrepreneur, for this elegant summer recipe.

1 clove garlic
¼ c olive oil
1 lb young zucchini
½ c pine nuts
¼ lb Pecorino Romano or Parmigiano-Reggiano
black pepper

1. Smash the garlic and let it rest in the olive oil for about 20 minutes.
2. Peel the zucchini, leaving small strips of green or yellow skin for some color. Discard most of the skin. For shorter ribbons, first cut each zucchini in half. Continue to peel the zucchini, creating thin ribbons of flesh, until you get down to the seeds. If the seeds are small, the shavings from the core are tender and tasty.
3. Remove the garlic from the oil and toss the zucchini with just enough oil to coat it lightly.
4. In a dry skillet, toast the pine nuts until they're just golden. Remove them from the hot pan.
5. Grate the cheese in thin ribbons like the zucchini.
6. Arrange the zucchini in a heap. Top it with the pine nuts, the cheese, and a grind of black pepper. Serve immediately at room temperature. ✛

cuban house salad

Serves 6

Michele Pulaski, who has cooked and eaten all over the Delaware Valley and beyond, orders this Cuban standard, which calls for lime juice and cilantro, at Martino's, in Somerville, New Jersey. After some home experiments, she cracked the recipe, made it her own, and gave it to me. I like orange juice in place of the lime. Use a sturdy lettuce—either romaine (or any cos type) or a French crisp type. It must hold up under the weight of the avocado. The riper the avocado, the less olive oil you'll need. In fact, Michele doesn't use any oil, but I can't resist. As the avocado falls apart, it adds a creamy texture—and fat—to the dressing.

1 orange or 1 lime
2-4 T olive oil
2 cloves garlic
1 head romaine (cos) or French crisp lettuce
1 red bell pepper
12 red globe radishes
2 ripe avocados
salt and pepper
cilantro to taste

1. Juice the orange to yield about 4 tablespoons or the lime to yield 2.
2. Put the juice into a bowl with half the olive oil.
3. Mince the garlic and add it to the dressing.
4. Chop the lettuce in generous chunks and put it in a large serving bowl.
5. Cut the peppers into thin strips and slice the radishes.
6. Peel the avocado and cut the flesh into chunks.
7. Add all the vegetables and the dressing to the lettuce and toss gently. The avocado will fall apart a little and become part of the dressing. Add more olive oil to taste. Season.
8. Chop the cilantro and scatter it on the salad.
Serve at once. ✣

iceberg and tomatoes with blue cheese dressing

Serves 4 generously

It was February at our country place in Hunterdon County, New Jersey, an old farmhouse on thirty-seven acres we call Small Farm, after Farmer Small in the Lois Lenski books of the 1940s. Rob went to the supermarket nearby for blue cheese. He couldn't bring himself to buy any of it, and in desperation, and uncharacteristically, he brought home a jar of lasts-forever blue cheese dressing. Perhaps it wasn't out of character; after forty years in the grocery and fine-food business, he always has the same question: Why on earth can't they make something good and simple and put it in a jar? Much of his shopping amounts to research; alas, the cloud of disappointment ever hovers. The poor fellow had looked at all the dressings and bought the only one without sugar. Its first ingredient was soybean oil; then blue cheese, milk, and eggs. It had the slightly acrid taste of stale spices, which I assume derived from the dried garlic and "natural" flavor. It was harsh and salty. Xanthan gum, an additive used to thicken many foods, made its appearance. Rob is prone to despair, but you needn't be. Way back, during a summer at the beach, we perfected blue cheese dressing, and it never disappoints. My present favorite blue is Chiriboga, a Bavarian cheese made by a Chilean who fell in love with a German. If you've given up on iceberg, look again. Iceberg grown on rich soil by a farmer who cares and sold fresh is much nicer than the supermarket kind.

½ lb blue cheese
4 T crème fraîche or sour cream
4 T milk
black pepper
chives or garlic chives (optional)
1 head iceberg lettuce
2-4 tomatoes

1. Bring the cheese to room temperature if you can.
2. Crumble the cheese in a medium-sized bowl to yield a generous cup.
3. Add the crème fraîche or sour cream and mash with a fork until it's mostly creamy, with chunks between the size of a pea and a blueberry.
4. Mix in the milk. If it is too thick for your taste, thin with more milk.
5. Grind in lots of fresh pepper and mix well.
6. Mince the (optional) chives and add them.
7. Dribble the dressing on a wedge of iceberg and large wedges of tomatoes. Do not toss; the dressing is heavy and no greens can take it. Serve at once. ✣

cobb salad

Serves 6

Cobb salad is a meal in itself, one that I cannot eat too often, and though it's humble, my diary tells me that I've made it many times for special guests and celebrations. It was the meal I served Rob and my mother after the movies on October 20, just days before Julian was born. But I associate it most with blistering summer days, when I can roast or poach the chicken in advance, assemble the salad at leisure in a cool kitchen, pour a glass of rosé, and have nothing to clean up after dinner. The next day, you can simmer the chicken bones in the poaching liquid and there will be extra dark meat for soup. A sturdy romaine and curvy Boston lettuce make the best bed of leaves; they have a lot to hold up. Cobb salad makes a beautiful buffet. On a hot June night for our occasional dinner-with-speaker series, Sundays at Six, we fed forty people who happily made their own salads in large bowls. You'll have more vinaigrette than you need.

1 large chicken or 3 large chicken breasts (bone in, skin on)

6 eggs

12 pieces bacon

1 head romaine

1 head Boston (Bibb) lettuce

2 tsp Dijon mustard

¼ c red wine or Champagne vinegar

1 c olive oil

salt and pepper

2 ripe avocados

½ lb crumbly blue cheese, such as Bayley Hazen by Jasper Hill Farm

1 pint cherry or grape tomatoes

You can prep these ingredients one day in advance and put them in the fridge:

1. Poach the chicken (page 90). If you're using chicken breasts, poach them just before serving the salad; they dry out quickly.

2. Put the eggs in cold water and bring it to a boil. Let them simmer on a low boil for 8 minutes, so the yolk is still dark yellow and a little moist in the middle. Cool.

3. Fry the bacon and drain it on paper towels.

4. Wash, spin, and drain the lettuces. Keep them in the salad spinner basket in the fridge.

5. Whisk the mustard and vinegar until smooth, and then dribble in the olive oil and whisk. Season with salt and pepper.

To assemble the salad:

1. Cut or hand-shred the chicken into bite-sized pieces, peel and halve the eggs, break up the bacon, peel and slice the avocados, crumble the cheese, and chop the tomatoes in half.

2. Tear the lettuce by hand.

3. Dress the leaves, tossing well, in a large kitchen bowl or, if it's big enough, in the serving bowl.

4. Scatter all the toppings on the salad. Don't toss it again. Serve in large bowls. ✢

egg salad

I love tangy crème fraîche in egg salad, but Rob thinks it's peculiar and prefers mayonnaise; see what you think. I also favor tiny green things in an egg salad. The vinegar is indispensable.

2 eggs per person
**1 T crème fraîche or mayonnaise (page 31) per egg–
or more if you like**
dill or parsley, finely chopped
a few scallions or chives, finely chopped
a few capers
sprinkle of Champagne vinegar or white wine vinegar
salt and pepper

1. Boil eggs as on page 29.
2. In a bowl, chop the eggs roughly with two butter knives or a pastry cutter.
3. Gently mix all the ingredients except the vinegar gently, keeping the eggs in discernible chunks.
4. Season with the vinegar to taste. Proceed cautiously and mix gently. Season. ✢

Mayonnaise

Makes about 8 tablespoons

Mayonnaise is an emulsion—a stable mixture of egg yolk, oil, and vinegar or lemon juice. Lecithin, an important nutrient for your brain found in egg yolks, is the emulsifier, the Great Joiner. I'm a fan of the food processor, but with mayonnaise, a bowl and a whisk give you more control—if you have the endurance—and this batch is too small for most machines. Whisking is less work if the bowl is deep and narrow. You will whisk without stopping for about twenty minutes, until soft peaks form. If the oil and vinegar don't marry, you'll have a thin, yellow sauce. A whisk can rescue split mayo. Crack a new yolk in a clean bowl and add the split mix to the yolk bit by bit, as if it were fresh oil. Most commercial mayonnaise, like the two pictured flanking mine, is made with sunflower or safflower oil, and it shares their bland flavor. With good olive oil, your mayonnaise will be greenish and peppery. According to Marion Trutter in *Culinaria Spain*, "Wherever olive oil existed, a simple preparation of oil and egg came about—particularly in the Mediterranean region, where aioli (oil and garlic) is made." If you don't care for green and peppery, try a yellow, buttery olive oil with a mild finish.

3 large egg yolks at room temperature
juice of ½ lemon
1 c olive oil
unrefined salt

1. In a bowl, whisk the yolks until they are smooth. Add the lemon juice and whisk to emulsify.
2. Add the oil in tiny spoonfuls, whisking all the while. Do not add more oil until the mayonnaise turns a shade paler than the yolks and begins to thicken. Whisk cautiously for about 10 minutes. You can add the oil a bit more quickly near the end. There is no need to use all the oil: too much oil makes for thin mayo.
3. Salt to taste. Use within 1 week. ✢

- -

Mustard Mayonnaise

Whisk in ½ teaspoon of Dijon mustard at the end.

Aioli

Dice and smash a small clove of garlic, mix it with a little olive oil, and slip that into the finished mayonnaise.

Herb Mayonnaise

Make a tiny batch of fresh green pesto (with, say, basil or tarragon) with olive oil. Whisk that into the finished mayonnaise. The effect will be smooth and intense.

deviled eggs

Serves any number

When I was little, we kept summer chickens. In the fall, we sent our laying hens away to become soup, and we continued to eat our own eggs, laid in the late summer and fall, for much of the winter. Not very fresh eggs, you think? But our eggs—even six, eight, or twelve weeks old—were still superior to supermarket eggs, partly because our chickens lived better than industrial layers: they ran free in the meadows behind the barn and under wild farm shrubbery, eating grass and bugs. This produces a deep yellow yolk, rich in vitamin A that the chicken makes from the carotenes in pastures, and rich in omega-3 fats that the chicken gets from bugs. Industrial yolks are pale yellow by comparison (see page 34). Our eggs stayed fresh for another reason: they wore a protective film, designed to keep the yolk fresh for the developing chick, a film we did not wash off. I still don't wash our own eggs, and I prefer to buy unwashed eggs from farmers, too, though in practice we eat them very quickly. Fresh eggs have one disadvantage, however: they don't peel easily. It has nothing to do with how you cook or cool them. When you want a perfectly smooth peeled egg, just use older eggs. Keep the eggs in the fridge for three or four weeks or at (a coolish) room temperature for a couple of days. They will still be plenty fresh and will peel easily. Say, how old are supermarket eggs, anyway? The expiration date must be no more than thirty days from the date the eggs were packed. Most eggs are packed within one week of being laid. So the typical store-bought egg may be a month old on the day you bring it home.

1 egg per person
1 T mayonnaise (page 31) or crème fraîche (or both) per egg
½ tsp Dijon mustard per egg
splash of olive oil to taste
salt
sprinkle of paprika
pinch of cayenne (optional)

1. Lay the eggs gently in cold water (if you start with cold water, they seem to crack less), bring it to a boil, turn down the heat, and simmer for 10 minutes.
2. Let the eggs cool and peel the shells carefully.
3. Cut the eggs in half in either direction and remove the yolk.
4. Mash the yolk with the mayonnaise or crème fraîche and the mustard. I like a little olive oil, too. Make it perfectly smooth. Salt to taste.
5. Fill the whites with the yolk mixture and sprinkle with paprika. Those who want the cayenne pepper know who they are. ✛

cobb salad deviled eggs

Cobb salad in a mouthful, minus the chicken breast. Buy a small head of romaine or Bibb-type lettuce, such as buttercrunch, which is strong enough to carry itself upright.

deviled eggs (page 37)
bacon
cherry tomatoes
crumbly blue cheese
1 head sturdy lettuce such as romaine or buttercrunch

1. Mix and fill the eggs.
2. Fry and break up some bacon.
3. Chop the cherry tomatoes in half, crumble the blue cheese, and tear up the lettuce.
4. Top the deviled eggs with the lettuce, bacon, cherry tomatoes, and little nuggets of cheese. ✣

sauce gribiche

Serves 4 to 6

This classic French sauce, best at room temperature, is almost like a spoonful of rich salad. It's a delicious, coarse vinaigrette for topping sautéed chicken breast, wild salmon, or poached halibut. One warm day, Jacob and I ate our gribiche on boiled broccoli and then straight, with a spoon. It's also nice on sliced boiled potatoes and asparagus and makes a great filling for boiled eggs. This recipe is friendly to tinkering. If you really love cornichons, capers, or certain herbs, you cannot go far wrong by adding more to taste.

2 eggs

2 tsp Dijon mustard

½ c olive oil

2 tsp red wine vinegar

2 cornichons

2 tsp capers

3 T minced parsley (or chervil or tarragon or even dill)

salt and pepper

1. Lay the eggs gently in cold water, bring it to a boil, turn down the heat, and simmer for 10 minutes. Allow the eggs to cool.
2. Separate the whites and yolks. Mash the yolk with the mustard until smooth.
3. Dribble in the olive oil little by little. Beat it with a fork or whisk until it's smooth.
4. Add the vinegar and whisk.
5. Dice the egg white and cornichons into pea-sized cubes.
6. Add the egg whites, cornichons, capers, and herbs. Mix gently but well.
7. Season and serve at room temperature. ✚

In a dual tradition family, we are blessed by seasonal spiritual festivals twice as often. Easter we celebrate in the clutch of spring. We leave colorful eggs for the Easter bunny, who hides the eggs indoors and out and leaves chocolate for us.

think like a chef

Emily Duff

The last line in many restaurant recipes is "Finish with butter." A good trick it is, too. Butter brings flavor, texture, color, and shine to the dish. There is no shortcut and no substitute for this particular instruction, which the pros also render as "Mount with butter." Vegans could mount with olive oil, I suppose, but the effect will be more slippery than silky. The uses of butter had me thinking about all the things chefs know and we don't. So I asked my friend Emily, who spent twenty years in restaurant, pub, and café kitchens in New York City, to tell me how the professionals think about food and why. —NP

Some of the best home cooking I ever did professionally was at my farm-to-table café, Henrietta's Feed and Grain. Each morning I'd head to one greenmarket or another, come back laden, and write a fresh menu. I might make a starter of smoked bluefish from the small boats captained by Alex Villani, a wry waterman with iconic white hair and a beard. Perhaps there'd be a peach salad, roast chicken with herbs, a brambleberry crumble. The next day's dishes would be entirely new. Now the only hot, tiny kitchen I occupy is my own. It lacks the gadgets and staff I once relied on— and it's often overrun by twig sculptures, action figures, and small hungry people— but I still arrange it and run it like a professional kitchen. I still think like a chef.

We shop and cook seasonally. This saves money, keeps us creative, and lets local farmers do some of the kitchen work. If the raw beets have great flavor, so will the roasted beets we send to the table.

We talk to producers and purveyors, from farmers to butchers to chocolate makers. This gets us out of the kitchen to meet—and learn from—experts and like-minded foodists who share our passion for real food.

We use lesser-known cuts of meat, and we use the entire animal. The filet and tenderloin can be boring and expensive. We like shanks, hocks, cheeks, hanger, liver, kidney, chuck, and sweetbreads for deep and diverse flavors and great value.

We make stock from bones. A supply of meat and fish stock in the fridge and freezer lends big flavor when you need it. We like broth to moisten pasta, to give a little backbone to a quick soup, to braise root vegetables, to enhance a silky sauce.

We experiment daily, with everything from ingredients to tricks and techniques. We learned classic pairs and methods for good reason, but inventions keep them fresh. Once, not too long ago, no one had heard of Parmigiano ice cream with balsamic syrup.

We keep our tools clean and sharp: sharp knives and new blades keep us moving forward. Dull knives cause accidents. We buy a good knife and take care of it.

We respect primitive technology. Fire is our main tool. A well-seasoned cast-iron skillet is better than any nonstick pan, and cheaper, too.

We improvise freely. A recipe is merely an inspiration. Make it your own.

We prep and organize. We wash, peel, pick, blanch, chop, label, and store ingredients so they are ready to cook. We keep essential pantry items like unrefined sea salt and good olive oil fresh and handy. We make lists for shopping and prepping.

We taste as we cook—a must!

We are careful. We chop ingredients to a precise and identical shape and size for equal cooking time, season meats and fish before cooking, we sauté onions, shallots, then garlic—in that order. (Like you, we have burned the garlic a few times.)

We are patient. We babysit the chicken stock by skimming off the scum, get good color on meat before putting it in the oven, let the roast rest before slicing, sauté mushrooms in batches so we don't overcrowd the pan, slowly and luxuriously spoon-bathe fish in brown butter for silkiness.

We are thrifty. We save skillet scrapings for gravy, bones for stock, bacon fat for roast spuds, shrimp shells for stock, cheese rinds for soup, soured raw milk for baking, beet and turnip greens for sautéing, herb stems for aromatics.

We reduce for flavor. We simmer down meat and fish stock into a thick bit of demi-heaven, balsamic vinegar into a syrupy delight, and fresh juices into syrups for sodas and sauces.

We mount with butter. Say no more.

shaved fennel, apple, and radish salad

I will never make this winter salad in exactly this fashion again. And that is the cast-iron rule about cooking: a recipe is not a commandment; it is a record of something someone once cooked. And perhaps another person ate, perchance enjoyed. Your task: to go to the market in deepest February and find distinctive, crunchy things like watermelon radish, fennel, and apples and to make them look and taste lovely. They are not shy ingredients, so shave them as thinly as you possibly can.

1 orange
olive oil
salt and pepper
watermelon radish
fennel
green and red apples
chives or parsley
walnuts

1. Juice the orange. Whisk a dressing using four parts olive oil to one part juice. Season.
2. Shave the radishes, fennel, and apples in very thin slices on a mandolin.
3. Mince the herbs.
4. Toss it all, coating the vegetables thoroughly with the dressing.
5. Scatter walnuts on top. ✛

caesar salad

Serves 4 to 6

Each time I scan a Caesar salad dressing recipe, I have some quarrel with the method (you must rub the bowl with garlic) or ingredients (steak sauce). It's not that mine is better or more traditional—it's just the way I like it: mild garlic, assertive cheese, ample pepper. Of course this recipe is just begging for your adjustments. Over many years, I've used dried anchovies packed in salt, which are considered superior, and anchovies packed in olive oil, but I'm afraid I can't tell the difference in any recipe. I do love the mild white kind.

2 cloves garlic
¾ c olive oil
6 anchovies
1 lemon
1 egg
¼ lb Parmigiano-Reggiano
½ tsp Dijon mustard
black pepper
1 large head romaine lettuce
skillet herb croutons (recipe follows)

1. Peel the garlic and let the cloves rest in the olive oil for about an hour.
2. Rinse the anchovies (whether packed in salt or in oil). Dice and then mash them with a fork.
3. Juice the lemon to yield 2 tablespoons.
4. Separate the yolk from the white and set aside the white for another use. (I tip the extra white into the scrambled eggs the next morning.)
5. Grate the Parmigiano on the finest grater hole.
6. Whisk the anchovies, yolk, lemon juice, and mustard thoroughly.
7. Remove the garlic cloves from the olive oil and drizzle the oil into the egg mixture, whisking steadily to make an emulsion.
8. When the dressing is smooth, add half the cheese and lots of fresh black pepper.
9. Tear the lettuce in small pieces and toss the leaves thoroughly with the dressing. Sprinkle the rest of the grated Parmigiano on the lettuce and toss again so the cheese sticks nicely all over the leaves. Give it one more grind of pepper, scatter the croutons on top, and serve. ✢

skillet herb croutons

Fresh bread works as well as stale bread and tastes better, but if it's very moist, you might toast it before cubing it. Find a real, dense, yeasty loaf. If the bread is wimpy rather than substantial, the croutons simply won't be as good. Make the croutons no later than the morning of the day you serve the salad. In the winter, a tasty alternative to fresh herbs (I never use dried) is a dusting of cayenne or black pepper. You can also toss the bread cubes in the olive oil and herbs and bake them at 450°F.

1 slice of bread per person
parsley or chives
1 clove garlic
1-2 T olive oil per slice

Cut the bread in fairly neat cubes. The crust is optional. Mince the herbs and peel the garlic. Cut the clove in quarters. Heat the olive oil over low heat, add the herbs and garlic, and cook them gently until the oil is infused. Add the bread cubes and let them color on each side. If they get too dry, add more oil. Do not burn the garlic; pick the pieces out if they're getting brown. When the bread cubes are crispy, lift them out and let them drain and cool on a paper towel.

mediterranean salad

Serves 4 to 6

You'll see this dish with raw asparagus, but I prefer the green spear blanched for about two minutes in salted water. It's up to you. Fat or thin, it doesn't matter, as long as the farmer has picked it at peak maturity and it's fresh. The little scales at the tip should be tight to the stalk without being too tight, which means it's too young. If they are springing out, it's overmature. When there's no asparagus, try another rich green, like deeply crinkled spinach. No feta? Use black olives.

½ lb asparagus

1 head romaine or other French crisp lettuce

3 oranges

1 red onion

¼ lb feta

olive oil

salt and pepper

1. Boil salted water. Slice the asparagus in 2-inch pieces on a sharp diagonal and blanch it for about 2 minutes. Drain.
2. Cut the lettuce into generous pieces.
3. Peel the oranges and remove the pith. Section the oranges for the salad over a bowl so you can save the juice that dribbles.
4. Slice the onion in slivers.
5. Crumble the feta.
6. Toss it all with olive oil and the orange juice. Season. ✛

tomatoes & burrata

Serves 8

There is nothing to it. Find good tomatoes, good burrata, good olive oil, and fresh basil. Place the burrata in the center of a big platter. Slice the tomatoes and arrange them around the pouch of creamy, lactic heaven. Dribble olive oil over everything. Slice open the cheese just before serving. Serve with a large fork and large spoon to handle the tomatoes and the milky dressing (photo on page 22).

german potato salad
Serves 6 to 8

The flavors are standard: the plain spuds, the meaty bacon, the tangy cider vinegar, the spicy mustard. My only change is cooking the onions; I don't care for raw onions, and I love the way griddled onions taste with potatoes and bacon. Buy a good thick bacon from a maker like Nueske's or Surry Farms, which makes a slab bacon from Berkshire pork. One thing you must do with German potato salad: serve it at room temperature (photos on next two pages).

2 lbs waxy potatoes
olive oil
½ lb good thick bacon
1 onion
2–3 scallions
3 T cider vinegar
1 T dijon mustard
6 T olive oil
salt and pepper

1. If the potatoes have thin and lovely skin, don't peel them. Cut the potatoes in chunks to suit you, and boil them in cold salted water until just tender. Coat the potatoes with a little olive oil and set them aside. (You can do this one day ahead.)
2. Dice the bacon into small cubes and sauté it until it's as crispy as you like it; I like it softer. Drain. Strain the fat and keep it. (You can fry the bacon the day before and keep it covered in the fridge.)
3. Slice the onion thin and fry it in a little bacon grease.
4. Dice the scallions, both the green and white parts.
5. Whisk the vinegar and the mustard. Add the olive oil. Add a little warm bacon grease. Fiddle with the amount of vinegar and mustard if necessary, and season to taste.
6. Toss all the ingredients gently. ✢

green salad with walnuts, blue cheese, & champagne dressing

Serves 8

I'm afraid I cannot lose the notion that my dinner party is incomplete without a green salad. In darkest December, I bought the leaves for this salad to celebrate the birthday of our friend Paco from two of my favorite local farms: Bodhitree Farm, which spans sixty-five acres of preserved farmland in the Jersey Pinelands, and one of Paco's favorite farms, Queens County Farm, which sits on New York City land that has been farmed without interruption since 1697. It's a grown-up salad: a little bitter, crisp, acidic—just right for the unctuous Coq au Vin (page 97). If you're drinking Champagne or Prosecco, add a dash to this dressing for what Michele Pulaski calls the "bite and sparkle" of the real thing.

1 shallot
olive oil
Champagne vinegar
½ tsp honey
salt and pepper
2 large heads lettuce or 1 lb loose leaves
¼ lb fairly dry blue cheese, such as Rogue River blue cheese or Bayley Hazen from Jasper Hill Farm
½ c walnuts, raw or brined and roasted (page 21)

1. Mince the shallot as tiny as you can.
2. Whisk 2 parts olive oil to 1 part vinegar. Add the honey and season.
3. Dress and toss the leaves in a large, pretty bowl.
4. Crumble the cheese. Top the salad with the cheese and walnuts without mixing them into the greens. ✣

tongue salad

Serves 6

Before he became a fine sausage maker, my friend Stanley Feder of McLean, Virginia, was a senior CIA analyst. Now his company, Simply Sausage, makes more than thirty wonderful sausages with natural meats and fresh spices, using original recipes inspired by all the great sausage cultures—and by a few I didn't know were great. As well as making countless links in his own kitchen, Stan did old-fashioned apprenticeships with famous sausage-making families from Catalonia, Spain, to Vancouver. (Behold how a man who could forecast the political weather of a small country approaches the creation of a food start-up.) Stan is also one of those charming, apron-wearing, multiple-course dinner party gents, with good taste in wine and anecdotes. Here's his tongue salad, the kind of old-fashioned, timeless dish a cook like Stan probably never stopped making. Beef, veal, or ox tongue (sometimes called lengua) is an affordable cut underappreciated in both culinary and nutritional terms. Three ounces of tongue contains more than 40 percent of the daily recommended dose of vitamin B12 and nearly a quarter of the recommended zinc, plus vitamins B2 and B3, selenium, and iron.

1 medium veal tongue
a few cloves
a few black peppercorns
1 bay leaf
sprinkle of unrefined sea salt
3 T cider vinegar
1 scant T Dijon mustard
¾ c (12 T) olive oil
small handful of tarragon, parsley, or chives
1 large head of lettuce
a few stronger leaves of radicchio, endive, or dandelion

1. Boil the tongue in cold water for 10 minutes. Skim off the foam.
2. Add the cloves, peppercorns, bay leaf, and salt.
3. Continue boiling the tongue until it's tender, about 2 hours. Add more water if necessary.
4. Remove the tongue, reserving the broth, and peel it while it's still warm.
5. Strain the broth and reduce it to about 6 tablespoons.
6. Whisk the vinegar with the mustard to emulsify.
7. Add 6 tablespoons of broth to the vinegar-mustard emulsion and enough olive oil to make a somewhat thick vinaigrette. (Twice as much oil as liquid is about right.) Whisk.
8. Chop the herbs and add them to the dressing. Season.
9. Slice the tongue the short way. Dress and toss the salad, reserving a little dressing.
10. Lay the tongue over the leaves and pour the reserved dressing on the meat. ✢

soups

Chicken Stock

Beef Stock ÷ Demi-Glace

Fish and Shrimp Stock ÷ Vegetable Stock

A Bean Soup for Vegans

Coconut Chicken Soup ÷ Pea Soup with Mint

Cream of Corn Soup with Red Pepper Sauce

Wild Nettle Soup ÷ My Tomato Soup

Summer Chili

bone stocks

Bone broth is a basic ingredient of good cooking worldwide. Bone broths lend flavor, moisture, texture, and complexity to soups, sauces, grains, and gratins. Perhaps the most essential quality of broth is the presence of umami. The complex and tasty flavor of European and Asian broths is a product of a variety of amino acids from bones, meats, and vegetables. We now know that the first food of humans—breast milk—is also rich in the amino acids responsible for umami.

The frugal cook in particular understands the value of broth. Stock makes use of the odd bits of the animal: cartilage, neck bones, knuckles, feet. Although stock provides little if any complete protein, it is a "protein stretcher," meaning that it helps the body efficiently use available protein. That's why stock is a staple of protein-poor cuisines, and why the ration-era Bovril ads in Britain featured a cow made of vegetables. The (accurate) implication is that a bit of Bovril—essentially, reduced beef stock—could stretch even vegetables into something that resembles a steak.

Bone broth is also good for what ails you. Stock is traditionally on the menu for convalescents for its nutrients, digestibility, and immune-boosting properties. Broth itself is easy to digest and even improves digestion in two ways. First, the long boiling of collagen (the connective tissue in joints) creates gelatin, a soft, protein-rich food. Gelatin is a hydrophilic colloid, a water-loving agent that aids digestion. Second, the minerals in broth float in an electrolyte solution, an easy-to-digest form.

Vegetarians note that eating excess protein leaches calcium. (Eating sugar leaches even more calcium.) But bone stock provides calcium and other nutrients including phosphorous, magnesium, potassium, sulfate, and fluoride. The lesson here is simple: eat the whole beast. If you enjoy the muscle, be sure to savor the joints.

To what do we owe the magic of broth? The simple act of simmering—often aided by a small quantity of acid, such as wine—extracts the essential minerals from bone, cartilage, and marrow. Other flavors (from the meat left on the bone, the vegetables, or aromatics such as bay leaf) add to the complexity. Finally, reduction itself—removing water—yields intensity. Four rules apply to all stocks.

+ Start with cold water—a "cold boil."
+ Simmer, do not boil.
+ Skim any foam.
+ Leave the pot uncovered.

Why skim the gray foam? For the simple reason that it's not delicious. The foam is technically a mass of soluble cell proteins, and I suspect there's some junk in it, because the meat and bones of store-bought, industrial animals produce a lot more ugly foam than do the meat and bones of clean-living pastured animals. When I simmer a pastured chicken, the foam is white as snow.

Harold McGee, the science-minded author of *On Food and Cooking*, neatly explains the four rules of good stocks, and they mostly concern said foam. The cold start and low heat "allow the soluble proteins to escape the solids and coagulate slowly, forming large aggregates that rise to the surface," where you can easily remove them. A hot start and fast boil, by contrast, create "many separate and tiny particles that remain separate and cloud the stock." We leave the pot uncovered for related reasons: to cool the surface of the stock, reducing the likelihood of boiling; to dry out the foam, making it easier to skim; and to allow the water to evaporate, hastening the reduction that is the fundamental purpose of broth.

Whether you make proper veal, beef, poultry, and fish stock at home or buy it from a good butcher or a small farm, a supply of broth in your fridge and freezer will make you a better cook. Good bone broth is the ne plus ultra of convenience food.

Chicken Stock

Chicken soup is known as the Jewish penicillin for its ability to fight infections. Poultry fat is rich in monounsaturated palmitoleic acid, an antimicrobial fatty acid. There is no need to remove the skin before making stock. If you chill the stock and skim the layer of fat, just save that precious schmaltz for another use. You can freeze stock in small containers and use it to moisten rice or thin a sauce. Mine is usually fresh in the fridge; we make a big soup and drink a lot of flavored broth when it's around.

Classic Chicken Stock

Use backs, necks, and legs (all with the skin on), a peeled carrot, a stalk of celery, and a peeled onion. Pour cold water over the meat and aromatics. Simmer, but do not boil, for up to 6 hours, adding more water if necessary. From time to time, skim off the foam.

Poached Chicken Stock

This yields a nice clear broth, good for matzo ball soup, chicken soup, and for thinning light dishes such as pea soup. Poach a whole chicken in cold water with a peeled carrot, a stick of celery, a bay leaf, and a few peppercorns for about 45 minutes, or until the chicken is cooked all the way through. (Poke it with a skewer.) Lift the chicken out; strain and reduce the liquid by half or more. Skim off the foam the whole time, from poaching to reducing. Use the poached chicken for soup, chicken salad, Cobb salad, rice, or burritos.

Rustic Chicken Stock

Make a roast chicken and eat the meat. Remove any aromatics from the carcass, like garlic, lemon, or rosemary, and smash it up a little. Cover it with cold water and simmer for 1 hour or so, skimming off the foam. When the water is below the chicken, it's done. Strain. This broth will be darker, with a more intense flavor, than the Classic or Poached Chicken stocks.

Beef Stock

Buy knuckles and other joints for stock. Put a little olive oil in a baking dish and roast them at 300°F until they are brown all over, about 30 minutes. Put them in a large pot with an onion, a carrot, a celery stick, and (perhaps) a bay leaf, a few peppercorns, allspice, or star anise. Add a splash of wine, which provides the acidity to draw minerals from the bones. Cover the bones with cold water and simmer uncovered for 3 hours or more. Strain and chill the liquid. Skim the fat. Why? For a recipe like Beef Burgundy, I don't want to add a lot of extra fat—the meat will provide it. What I want from the stock is intense flavor and silky gelatin.

Demi-Glace

Demi-glace is a traditional French sauce made by combining reduced veal stock with a complex sauce called *espagnole* which I have never made. The real thing is very good, representing as it does the essence of beef, plus all the flavors (vegetal, herbal) in the recipe, and a generous spoonful or two makes all the difference in pot roast, brisket, and stews. But what a lot of work.

There are good options short of the full French method. You can buy good demi-glace. You can make a simple reduced beef stock. It won't have the complexity of demi-glace, but it will taste of beef and deliver the unctuous texture.

Poor Man's Demi-Glace

The title is mine. For a simple reduced beef stock, roast marrow and knuckle bones at 350°F until they're golden brown and crispy. Cover them with cold water and aromatics, simmer for at least 3 hours, and strain the broth. Repeat two more times with the same bones and fresh water and aromatics. Combine the broths and reduce to just a few cups.

Almost-Classic Demi-Glace

4-5 lbs marrow and knuckle bones

3 carrots

2 onions

olive oil

½ c tomato paste

1 bay leaf

2 thyme sprigs

1 c red Burgundy

1. Set the oven to 350°F.

2. In a pan that can go from oven to stove-top, bake the bones until they're golden-brown and crispy, about 45 minutes.

3. Peel the carrots and onions and cut them in large chunks. Dress them lightly with the olive oil.

4. Take the bones out and smear them with the tomato paste.

5. Put the vegetables and bones back in the pan, give it a shake, and bake for another 30 minutes or so, until the

vegetables have colored and the tomato paste is crispy and caramelized.

6. Take the bones out. Put the bones, vegetables, bay leaf, and thyme in a large, fresh pot, cover with cold water, and cook over low heat for about 15 minutes.

7. Meanwhile, put the roasting pan back on the burner, add the wine, scrape up all the delicious brown bits with a wooden spoon, and reduce the liquid. The scraping is called deglazing, and it's essential to the flavor of demi-glace.

8. Pour the reduced wine and every little scraping into the stockpot with the bones. Simmer uncovered over low heat. Do not boil. Reduce it as much as you dare; 8 hours is not too long. The density of the sauce is not important; a tablespoon of thick demi-glace is as good as a cup of a thinner one.

9. Strain the sauce, discard the bones and aromatics, and chill.

10. When it's cold, remove the solid fat. Demi-glace will stay fresh for 2 weeks in the fridge and freezes well. ✢

Fish & Shrimp Stock

Use fish stock as a base for a soup of shellfish or chunky white fish. It's also good for poaching a larger piece of fish. Ask the fishmonger for a pound of white fish bones and scraps—no heads, and no oily pink or red fish like salmon or tuna. Slice an onion and one celery stalk in thin pieces. Consider adding a few peppercorns and a bay leaf. Cover the fish, vegetables, and any aromatics with cold water and simmer for 30 to 40 minutes, skimming off any foam; it should be clear, not milky. Strain. To make fish fumet—a concentrated broth— simply reduce the strained stock by at least half. I also like stock made from wild spot prawns. If a recipe calls for peeling the prawns, I simmer the shells and tails in cold water for about 20 minutes and often use the stock on the spot to moisten the dish. When I'm serving prawns in their shells, I save the shells and tails and freeze the stock.

Vegetable Stock

"A flavorful stock is the key to successful vegetarian cooking." Those words are borrowed, but I'm familiar with the theory and subscribe to it. Strict vegan cooking–lacking, as it does, various animal-based options for depth and variety of flavor–can use the extra oomph. But not all vegetables yield good stock, and not all vegetables work well together. The statement I've quoted above was followed by a recipe for vegetable broth calling for ingredients that closely resemble the contents of my compost pile and conjure up similar odors. So let's start with plants that don't belong in the stockpot: eggplant and potato peels (both bitter), asparagus (slimy), chard (green broth, sulfurous when boiled), scallions (slimy when boiled), fresh tomatoes (mostly water and skin), and pea pods (all fiber, no flavor). Some intense characters, like carrots, winter squash, garlic, parsley, and fresh bay leaf, are welcome only in small numbers. Others make a wonderful one-note stock when applied to their own kind. For example, you might sauté sliced fennel, simmer it, and strain it for a broth to deepen the flavor of a fennel risotto. In general, minimalism is your ally. This simple broth makes all the difference in any vegetable soup. I've used it to thin creamy pasta sauce. And it's lovely on its own.

Makes about 1 quart

2 white onions
1 carrot
1 celery stalk
1 small thyme, rosemary, or parsley branch
1 fresh bay leaf
3 or 4 peppercorns
¼–½ c olive oil
unrefined sea salt

1. Chop the vegetables in chunks of any roughly equal size.

2. In a large pan, sauté everything in the olive oil until quite soft. Neither stint on the olive oil nor begrudge the time spent stirring. Fat, not water, carries flavor.

3. Cover with 2 quarts of cold water and simmer uncovered for about 30 minutes. Beware a fresh bay leaf–it is much more piney than a dry one and leaves a strong imprint. You might take it out after 15 minutes or so. Treat the herbs with care, too.

4. Strain and salt to taste. ÷

a bean soup for vegans

Serves 4 generously or 6 to start

A vegan diet has significant nutritional gaps, but I'm quite fond of meals made exclusively from plants. So fond that I often eat a meal made purely of roots, stems, leaves, sprouts, and seeds. I've even written a vegan café menu—a list of dishes to tempt the dullest carnivore. What I don't care for is bad, phony, and misguided dishes made of plants, like nut "cheese" and soy "chicken." So here is a delicious bean soup to make for the vegans you love. It's true that many who taste this soup, shortly after praising it, say, "That would be delicious with a shower of Parmigiano." Ah, the taste for protein. But don't let that stop you. If you first make a lovely vegetable broth, the vegans will feel well-fed. Any number of vegetables would be happy here. In winter, add a peeled, diced potato or carrot when you add the broth; in summer, add sautéed zucchini or griddled red peppers (both diced) with the garlic.

2 c dry beans such as cannellini, yellow eye, orca, cranberry, or Jacob's cattle

1 onion

¼ c olive oil plus more for drizzling

1 16-oz can whole peeled tomatoes or 4 fresh ripe Roma tomatoes

1 qt vegetable stock (page 57)

2 cloves garlic

small handful of rosemary, basil, or thyme

1 bay leaf

½ tsp salt

parsley to serve

1. Rinse the beans, soak them in fresh water for 3 to 5 hours, and drain. (Cayuga Pure Organics has advice on fresh and dry heirloom beans; you may want to precook them in unsalted water and then make the soup, depending on the variety and how fresh they are. There is nothing worse than overcooking and reducing your broth just to get the beans tender.)

2. Dice the onion. Heat some olive oil in a large pot and sauté the onion until it's soft.

3. Chop the tomatoes. Add the stock, tomatoes, and beans to the pot. Bring to a boil and simmer for about 30 minutes.

4. Meanwhile, dice and briefly sauté the garlic and herbs in a little olive oil in a small pan. The garlic should be white (not browned) and half-soft.

5. Add the garlic, herbs, bay leaf, and salt to the soup and cook until the beans are tender. Don't hesitate to add more water or broth; the beans must be just right.

6. Season and garnish with minced parsley and a drizzle of olive oil. ✢

chicken soups

Rob loves many dishes that I don't know how to cook and may never. Barbecue. Double-layer chocolate cake. Fried chicken. Blueberry pie. But when he first asked for chicken soup, long before we had children, I set to work without a recipe and with confidence. I poached a large pastured chicken with celery, carrot, onion, a few peppercorns. I strained the stock and reduced it; stripped and diced choice breast meat and thigh; diced and sautéed onion, carrot, and parsley in olive oil. Then I layered the stock, chicken, vegetables, and herbs in a pan to simmer. With a few minutes to go, I tossed in a handful of fresh shell peas, and finally, a sprig of dill. Rob took a spoonful. "It doesn't taste like my mother's."

He said the same of my first brisket and chopped liver. The chopped liver recipe, which I followed faithfully, I found in the famous *Second Avenue Deli Cookbook*, back when we used to eat at the beloved Jewish diner and it was actually on Second Avenue. The brisket recipe, which I followed less faithfully because of insuperable objections to certain ingredients, was handed to me with this title: Florence Kaufelt's Brisket.

Born in 1918, Florence Willner Kaufelt was a formidable, elegant, self-made, bookish woman whose uncensored wit and personal realpolitik Rob shares and frequently invokes. Though I knew her only briefly, her spirit fills the air, and on my dresser sits a large vintage bottle of her Ivoire de Balmain scent. The scents of her cooking, however, do not fill the kitchen. The person responsible for the cherished fried chicken and blueberry pie—recipes I dare not attempt—was Cora, the housekeeper-turned-cook of Rob's small-town boyhood.

My chances of matching the memory of Florence and Cora in the kitchen are slim. It is easier to be myself, and—perhaps more to the point—it is something of a necessary evil. Happily, I'm making my slow way toward proficiency. Rob has patiently taught stubborn me about proper cuts of meat, which, unfortunately, the butchers of some grass-farmers still don't seem to grasp. Michele Pulaski, a talented and self-taught cook who has become my friend, showed me how to make brisket, the piece of Jewish home cookery of which I was most gun-shy. (WASPS make pot roast, and I couldn't even cook that.) Michele's brisket shuns onion soup powder and Coca-Cola, two ingredients that haunt lesser versions. The clincher in this classic slab of falling-apart beef is a serious demi-glace.

Several years after polishing my chicken soup story, a symbol of my education in the kitchen and in the small stumbling blocks of wife-life, I picked up a memoir concerning Rob's relatively recent past. It was no secret that he'd had another life, in another kitchen, with another food writer. It seems that one day, when Rob was feeling poorly, she labored over a handmade chicken soup. Her method was eerily similar—the words might've been my own—and she presented the soup with equal confidence. "It doesn't taste like my mother's," he said. Clearly, she was talking about the man I knew.

A couple of years later, on a hot June night in New York City, I poached a six-pound chicken in water with salt, peppercorns, and a bit of olive oil, for a solid hour, producing a nice broth. I sautéed bulb spring onions, uncured garlic, thin coins of young carrots, and lots of parsley, all from the market. The chicken breasts were huge, so I coated one with olive oil and put it away for chicken salad, and I shredded the other. The thigh meat was nice and went in. I poured the hot broth into a large bowl over the moist meat and soft vegetables and gave it a twist of salt and of pepper. I shared the soup with Julian, who was three, and with Jacob and Rose, who were not quite one year old. After I put them to bed, Rob came home from the studio, where he was making a record called *Sweet Virginia Girl*. I sat with him while he chatted about his new songs, ate No Recipe Chicken Soup, and murmured his approval. In August we were married.

coconut chicken soup

Serves 8

One of the few vegetable oils that is highly saturated, coconut oil has been accused of raising cholesterol and contributing to heart disease. But coconut oil does not raise blood cholesterol in unhealthy ways. It does raise HDL (high-density lipoprotein), and according to the National Heart, Lung, and Blood Institute, "the higher your HDL cholesterol level, the lower your chance of getting heart disease." In tropical countries where unrefined coconut oil is eaten liberally and the diet still consists of traditional foods, heart disease is rare. Coconut milk is also rich in lauric acid, the antiviral fatty acid found in breast milk (and required, by law, to be in infant formula), which gives newborns immunity. Calories notwithstanding, coconut oil won't make you fat. The body burns the short- and medium-chain fatty acids in coconut oil first, before long-chain fatty acids such as those in vegetable oils and fish oil, which it prefers to store. Because it's stable at high temperatures, coconut oil is excellent for cooking and baking. The coconut and chicken broth make this luscious soup the ultimate cold-and-flu therapy. A ratio of three cups of stock to one cup of coconut milk makes a perfect creamy soup, or you can make a lighter one by adding more stock. Don't buy "light" coconut milk, which is diluted with water. If you buy ginger but don't use it up quickly, keep a large root sealed in plastic bag in the freezer, and hack off a thumb-sized piece when you need it.

1 thumb-sized knob of fresh ginger
1 lemon
6 c chicken stock
4 c (2 14-oz cans) unsweetened coconut milk
1 tsp chili pepper flakes
¼ tsp unrefined sea salt
cilantro, scallions, garlic chives, or Thai basil to garnish

1. Grate (but do not peel) the ginger on the smallest grater hole.
2. Juice the lemon to yield about 1 tablespoon.
3. Heat the chicken stock. Skim off any foam.
4. Add the ginger, lemon juice, coconut milk, chili flakes, and salt.
5. Simmer for 10 minutes. Season and garnish. ✧

pea soup with mint

Serves 4

What is tastier than fresh shell peas from the farmers' market in June? I'll tell you what's tastier. Frozen peas from some huge, far-away organic farm. My parents taught us with a firm hand how to pick peas. The size and shape, texture and color of the shell must be just so, or the peas will be too small (and bland) or too big (and starchy). But I never find such perfect peas at local markets. They're always tough and starchy. Is there any hope for local shell peas? Does anyone know how to pick them? Perhaps the trouble lies in the time between picking and market, when the precious sugars have turned to starch. In my day, sweet corn farmers ran a similar risk, but modern corn varieties hold their sugar much longer. Until a local farmer proves me wrong, I'm not serving local peas. Happily, frozen industrial organic peas are very good. I buy them with impunity all year. This makes about 3 cups without the milk. That's a modest cup of soup for three people, but I usually make it with one bag of peas, so that's how I've written it. The recipe is easily doubled.

1 lb frozen green peas
2 shallots
4 T olive oil
2 c chicken stock
1 T crème fraîche plus more to garnish
1 dill sprig
1-2 c milk to taste (optional)
salt and pepper
mint to garnish

1. Cook the peas in boiling salted water for about 2 minutes.
2. Dice and sauté the shallots in about half of the olive oil until they're soft.
3. Put all the ingredients except the milk in a food processor and blend until smooth.
4. Taste and thin with the (optional) milk. Season.
5. For a perfectly smooth soup, strain it—the tiny pea coats are a bit grainy.
6. Garnish with more crème fraîche and mint. Serve warm or cold. ✢

cream of corn soup with red pepper sauce

Serves 8

It was September and we had lots of white corn left over from a big barbecue. It wasn't the best corn. We boiled it and ate it with butter—a marginal improvement. I cut the rest off the cob for soup. Feeling guilty about wasting bits on the cob, I hit on a solution. Simmer the cobs in milk! Perfect: the corn softened and expanded, releasing its flavor to the milk without the stringy bits. Then we salted and sucked on the milk-drenched cobs. I make this soup, or something quite like it, all year, with frozen corn and fresh. Other nice garnishes are minced chives or parsley and crème fraîche. This makes 2 quarts or 8 cups—a scant 8 servings; add milk, cream, or stock to thin it or to serve more.

2 lbs fresh or frozen sweet corn kernels

1 onion

4 T butter, olive oil, or a mix

2 c milk (plus more for thinning optional)

¼ c cider

½ tsp salt

cream or stock (optional)

ground cayenne

sweet bell pepper sauce or hot red pepper oil (recipes follow)

1. If you're using fresh corn, cut the kernels off the cob into a bowl, reserving any liquid. For more flavor, simmer the stripped cobs in the milk. If you're using frozen corn, defrost and drain the kernels.
2. Dice the onion.
3. In a large pot, heat the butter and/or olive oil and sauté the onion until it's quite soft.
4. Add the corn to the onion and sauté until it's just soft.
5. Add the milk, cider, and salt to the onions and corn. Cook until it simmers. Do not boil.
6. Whiz it all in the food processor and season with cayenne to taste. If the soup is too thick, thin it with more milk or (optional) cream or (optional) stock to taste.
7. Dribble a pepper sauce on the soup or serve it on the side. ✢

Sweet Pepper Sauce

Slice a sweet red pepper and sauté it in olive oil until very soft. Whiz in the food processor until it is completely smooth.

Hot Pepper Oil

Dice and gently sauté a hot red pepper in olive oil until it's soft but not brown. Let it sit in the oil for at least 1 hour. Strain. You can also whiz a raw hot pepper to make a nice thick orange oil. The flavor will be quite different.

wild nettle soup

Serves 4

Don't get foragers, herbalists, and midwives started on nettle tea. The leaves and tender stems of stinging nettles are rich in vitamins A and C, beta-carotene, calcium, iron, magnesium, and potassium. Nettles are said to ease arthritis, gout, and anemia; stimulate the liver and aid digestion; increase fertility, reduce labor pain, and stimulate breast milk production. Nettles grow enthusiastically by roads, streams, and woods in the spring. They are staples of poverty cooking wherever they grow. (I first saw nettle soup in *They Can't Ration These*, a wonderful wartime British cookbook.) The tiny stinging hairs leave a burning rash, which is temporary but painful. Wear gloves to gather and prepare them. The fresher the nettle, the sharper the sting. Boiling for 20 minutes renders the hairs mostly harmless, but if you're delicate, you may get a tickle in the throat from al dente nettle soup; if so, cook it longer. The longer you cook nettles, however, the duller the flavor and color; nutrients are lost too. In this soup, you can certainly use butter, but with grassy nettles, I prefer olive oil.

Diced boiled potatoes make a nice addition.

2 onions
¼ c olive oil
2 cloves garlic
½ lb nettle tops (the leaves and small, tender stems)
1 ½ qts vegetable broth, chicken or beef stock, or water
unrefined sea salt

1. Chop the onions, warm the olive oil, and sauté the onions until they're soft.
2. Chop the garlic, add it to the onions, and sauté briefly.
3. Add the nettles and cook until they're wilted. Add the liquid and simmer until the sting is gone but the nettles are still bright green—no more than 30 minutes. Drain the solids from the liquid, saving both. Purée the leaves and onions with a bit of broth until perfectly smooth.
4. Add more liquid to thin the soup to the consistency you prefer. Season. ✦

my tomato soup

Serves four (8-ounce cups)

It's nice to have some quick dishes in your repertoire, and tomato soup is finally one of mine. For too long, I would buy house-made tomato soup from nice local places only to quibble with it. Too smoky, too salty, too sweet, too pink, too lumpy. At last my indolence shamed me, so I bought a can of good Italian tomatoes and devised my kind of soup. This is a velvety number with a solid tomato character. It has the sweetness of carrots, the spice of celery, the nutty depth only butter can offer, and only a whisper of milk.

1 onion

2 celery stalks

2 small carrots

⅓ c olive oil

1 large clove garlic

1 qt jar or 28-oz can tomatoes

1 bay leaf

½ tsp salt

2 T unsalted butter

sprinkle of paprika

grind of black pepper

whisper of cayenne

1 c milk

crème fraîche (optional)

a good cracker, such as Whitney's Castleton, with Jasper Hill cheddar (optional)

1. Dice the onion and slice the celery and carrots in thin rounds. Heat the olive oil in a large pot and sauté the vegetables until soft.

2. Chop the garlic, add it to the vegetables, and sauté for a few minutes.

3. Add the tomatoes, bay leaf, and salt. Simmer for 10 minutes. A little water or a little more simmering would not go amiss.

4. Turn off the heat. Add the butter, paprika, black pepper, and cayenne.

5. Let the soup cool in the pot as long as you like. Remove the bay leaf and whiz the soup in the food processor until it's completely smooth.

6. Add the milk. Mix well or whiz briefly.

7. Garnish with the (optional) crème fraîche. ✢

summer chili

Serves 4

Why should chili always be a stick-to-your-ribs, cold-weather dish? The summer after I moved home from London, I worked for my parents at the Arlington and Dupont Circle farmers' markets. Gardener's Gourmet had fresh (that is, not yet dried) shell beans I liked. They were Appaloosa, a speckled kidney, and Dixie butter beans, resembling a red baby lima. Heirloom tomatoes, meanwhile, were cheap from our very own Wheatland Vegetable Farms. Dead-ripe and occasionally unsightly tomatoes—what we call seconds—were for sale by the gallon basket, for sauce, juice, salsa, soup. I made a summer chili with fresh beans and tomatoes and ate it cold with Latin American cultured sour cream, or *crema*, which is pourable, salty, and tasty. Buy *crema* at Latino supermarkets, or use sour cream or crème fraîche. One pound of beans makes a modest 4 portions of soup. Make enough tomato juice to cover the beans fully.

1 lb fresh red beans
3 lbs dead-ripe tomatoes
2 cloves garlic
¼ c olive oil
salt and pepper
crema, sour cream, or crème fraîche to garnish

1. Rinse and pick through the beans, removing withered ones and small stones.
2. Cut the stem ends off the tomatoes and chop roughly. Put the tomatoes in a food processor or blender and whiz until the juice is thick and smooth.
3. Peel and chop the garlic.
4. In a large pot, sauté the garlic in the olive oil until it's soft, being careful not to burn it.
5. Add the beans and tomato juice to the garlic.
6. Bring to a boil and simmer for 30 minutes or until the beans are tender.
7. Season and serve hot or cold with any cultured cream. ✢

family seder

matzo ball soup

leg of lamb with rosemary and garlic

fork-split roasted potatoes

the seder plate

charoset

flourless chocolate cake

matzo ball soup

Serves 8 to 10

Matzo ball: A dumpling made from ground matzo (unleavened) bread. Also (forgive me) a somewhat comic item, which nevertheless completes this lovely clear chicken soup for reasons sentimental, theological, and traditional. Don't attempt whole-meal matzo balls; they disintegrate like a fistful of sand. Bring the eggs to room temperature; if they are very cold, they might bind the butter. Speaking of butter, Michele Pulaski, who has cooked many more Seders than I have, convinced me that butter makes the matzo balls much better. It was not a hard sell. If your Seder is (correctly) dairy-free, use a half cup of olive oil.

1 large chicken
1 celery stalk
6 carrots
1 onion
peppercorns
matzo balls (recipe follows)
1 bunch dill or parsley
1 piece fresh horseradish

1. Poach a whole chicken (page 55) with the celery, 2 carrots, the onion, and a few peppercorns.
2. Strain the stock, discarding the aromatics. Tear off the wings of the chicken, put them in the stock, and reduce it by half. Strain it again. See that the broth has the right quality for a soup: neither too thick nor too watery. Thin or reduce it if necessary and season. Save 2 cups for poaching the matzo balls.
3. Slice the remaining carrots very thinly and boil them in salted water or the chicken stock.
4. Mince the dill or parsley.
5. Assemble each serving of soup in a shallow bowl. Put a couple of matzo balls and cooked carrots in first. Pour the clear broth—not the matzo-cooking broth—over the dumplings. Top with minced dill or parsley and grated horseradish. ✣

matzo balls

parsley

4 eggs

½ c sparkling water

1 c matzo meal

¼ c (½ stick, or 2 oz, or 4 T) unsalted butter

¼ c olive oil

2 c chicken stock

Mince the parsley. Whisk the eggs. Add the water to the eggs. Add the matzo meal to the egg mixture and mix. Melt the butter with the olive oil. Pour the fats into the matzo meal mixture. Mix well. Let the batter stand for 10 to 15 minutes. Mold 8 large or 16 small dumplings—one or two per person. Meanwhile, simmer the chicken stock. Boil the dumplings for 2 to 3 minutes. They will puff up and bob when they're ready.

leg of lamb with rosemary & garlic

Serves 8 to 10

I like that the culinary centerpiece–the sacrificial lamb–of the Seder meal matches the season. Many cooks serve brisket, but I prefer the symbolism of lamb, and I never promised you a traditional Seder. We always have a green salad at this meal, although it's not terribly traditional either, just to keep things light. The Seder plate is all about spring greens, so why not eat some?

5-6 lb leg of lamb

salt and pepper

olive oil

1 onion

2 cloves garlic

rosemary

parsley

1 c red wine

2 c demi-glace (page 56)

1. Set the oven to 350°F.
2. Rinse the lamb, pat it dry, and season all over.
3. In a large heavy pot, heat the olive oil and brown the lamb on as many sides as you can. Don't turn it until it colors. Take it off the heat.
4. Dice the onion, smash the garlic, and chop the herbs. Mash it all up with olive oil and plenty of salt and pepper on a cutting board to make a rough paste.
5. With a sharp knife, cut narrow slits in the lamb and jam the herb mixture in. Make some cuts right to the bone, but choose corners and edges; don't put holes right in the prime parts of the meat.
6. Roast the lamb for about 45 minutes, checking it after 30 minutes; grass-fed lamb will cook quickly. We like it medium-rare and tend to eyeball it, but if you prefer a thermometer, make it 120°F in two spots near the bone. Take the lamb out of the pan and keep the drippings. Spoon away any extra fat.
7. Pour the wine in the roasting pan with the drippings and reduce it by half on the stove.
8. Add the demi-glace and simmer.
9. The gravy is ready when the taste of wine is gone. Strain it, skim the fat, and season.
10. Set the lamb on a spike for carving and pass a bowl of gravy. ✥

fork-split roasted potatoes

Serves 8

Each spring I notice that there is something out of season about the typical Passover menu. In our region, April is really too early for new potatoes and young carrots. June is more like it. My local markets are full of storage roots, of course, but it seems a shame to buy last year's vegetables for a festival of fertility, freedom, and renewal. So I use just a slice or two of mature local carrots in the matzo ball soup, mostly because the orange is pretty, and then I prevaricate about the spuds. I could do without them entirely, but the dish is de rigueur. Whether you buy big storage potatoes, new potatoes (from Somewhere Else), or fingerlings, they will look and taste great if you fork-split them. Even a Yukon Gold—the ideal mashing potato—will taste great roasted. The raggedy surface grabs the butter and makes for tasty browned crevices. If the meal seems rosemary-heavy, scatter minced parsley on the hot spuds just before serving. Try the smooth-skinned, yellow-fleshed bintje ("ben-jee") potato, developed a century ago by a Dutch botanist–school teacher.

A bintje is neither exceptionally starchy nor waxy and perfect for this dish.

½ lb potatoes per person
1 medium bunch rosemary or parsley
1 T unsalted butter per person
1 T olive oil per person
chunky sea salt, such as Maldon or Jacobsen
1 small piece fresh horseradish

1. Set the oven to 350°F.
2. Boil a large pot of salted water.
3. Scrub, then peel or partially peel the potatoes. Peel only the bits that are thick, unsightly, or green (thus, likely bitter).
4. Quarter big tubers and halve the smaller ones.
5. Boil the potatoes until they are half-soft. Drain.
6. While the potatoes are cooking, mince the rosemary or parsley.
7. Stab the drained potatoes with a fork and work the tines back and forth to split them. Make the pieces large, chunky, and relatively even, but don't overdo it or you'll get many tiny bits.
8. Toss gently with the butter, olive oil, herbs, and salt.
9. Roast the potatoes in one layer until fork-tender and golden, about 30 minutes.
10. Grate fresh horseradish on the finest grater hole over the potatoes and serve hot. ✢

the seder plate

The best part of this seasonal ritual I've acquired by marriage is the Seder plate. It's both concrete and symbolic, both traditional and open to variation. The symbols are cultural, historical, political, and theological. The Seder plate consists of seasonal foods that are integral to the meal, rather than foreign and separate. It's simple, it's beautiful, and it's moving. A child can understand it.

My plate is simpler than most but honors the main themes.

Saltwater

Imagine seawater honored at a meal, rather than singing backup. You dip the boiled egg and the romaine in the saltwater. I put a small bowl on the Seder plate and a couple of small bowls on the table to pass.

Sweat and tears.
Ritual cleansing.
The passage through the Red Sea.

Charoset

Literally, the mortar. Clay, straw, and blood. My recipe is Ashkenazi and suits our northern clime. Sephardic Jews make chutney-like mixes with dried fruits such as figs and apricots.

The apples and nuts are the bricks.
The cinnamon stick is the straw in the mortar.
The wine is the blood of bondage.

Beitzah

A roasted egg. Mine is boiled for reasons of efficiency. A boiled egg on the plate can be the one you dip in saltwater and eat at the beginning of the meal.

Spring, new life, rebirth.
Ritual sacrifice.
A symbol of mourning for the destroyed temple.

Zeroah

A roasted lamb shank. Permissive interloper that I am, I often use a bone from the chicken stock made the day before; otherwise you're scraping and cleaning a lamb bone just before sitting down.

The ritual sacrifice of a spring lamb.
The birth of the lambs on the farms.
Mercy.

Maror

Literally a bitter herb. Horseradish is a newcomer—until the late sixteenth century, all the rabbis called for romaine. I use romaine (here) or fresh, grated horseradish.

The bitterness of slavery under the Pharaoh.

Karpas

This means parsley, but any green vegetable will do. In Eastern Europe many families use a potato. I use parsley, romaine, or any lettuce we're eating.

Green shoots.
Spring.

Matzo

Unleavened bread. Matzo is the most important symbol of Passover. The Ashkenazi recipe is like a cracker, but others are softer, like a Greek pita or a tortilla. When the Israelites left Egypt in haste, there was no time for bread dough to rise.

A humble reminder of life in slavery.
Redemption and freedom.

charoset

Serves 8 to 10

This Ashkenazi version feels more like a fall recipe, but it suits our northern region, and you'll just have to choose good storage apples. Use raw walnuts or brined and roasted ones (page 21). I like charoset slightly moist, hence all the liquid. I use a lot of cider in place of the red wine so children can eat as much as they like. Modify as you please.

2 c walnuts
4-5 apples
2 T sweetish red wine
4 T apple or pear cider
dusting of cinnamon
grind of salt
1 cinnamon stick

1. Chop the walnuts roughly.
2. Chop the apples in small, even pieces. Aim for 2 to 3 cups, chopped.
3. Toss the walnuts and apples with the wine, cider, ground cinnamon, and salt.
4. Add the cinnamon stick for its beauty and symbolism.
5. Serve at once, before the apples color. ✢

flourless chocolate cake

Serves 10

This chocolate treat became a family tradition on the very first taste. Another gift from Michele Pulaski, it is intense, molten in the middle, and a touch sweeter than my usual fare, but I wouldn't change anything, partly because the sugar does things to the texture that one doesn't want to spoil. I like it best in individual ramekins. Taking the cake from the pan without minor scrapes and bumps takes some practice. Serve it with cream whipped with a tablespoon or two of crème fraîche. In raspberry season, garnish with a few ripe ones. Leave any uneaten cake on the counter rather than in the fridge. At cool temperatures, the butter will harden, and it's tastier when it's a bit soft.

6 eggs

1 ⅓ c organic whole cane sugar

½ c water

2 bars (200 g or 7 oz) 100% chocolate

1 bar (100 g or 3.5 oz) 70% chocolate

1 c (2 sticks or 8 oz or 16 T) unsalted butter, softened

4 c heavy cream for whipping

4 T crème fraîche for whipping

1. Set the oven to 350°F.
2. Butter ten 4-ounce ramekins or a 9-inch springform cake pan. Choose a larger pan for a warm water bath.
3. In a bowl, whisk the eggs. Add ⅓ cup of the sugar and whisk until the mixture is fluffy, shiny, and almost meringue-thick.
4. In a saucepan, make a simple syrup with the remaining 1 cup of sugar and the water. Bring to boil and boil for exactly 2 minutes. Take off the heat.
5. Break the chocolate into small pieces and add them to the warm syrup. Stir gently until the chocolate has melted.
6. Add the butter to the chocolate. Blend gently. Let it cool slightly.
7. Fold the chocolate mixture into the eggs. Pour the batter into the ramekins or pan. Set in a bath of warm water and bake for about 30 minutes, or until a knife comes out clean.
8. Let the cake rest for 20 minutes. If it's in a pan, set it carefully onto a plate.
9. Meanwhile, whip the cream and crème fraîche. Garnish and serve. ✦

center of the plate

My Latest Poached Chicken

Thai Chicken Curry ÷ White Chicken Stroganoff with Dill

Moist Chicken with Rice ÷ Coq au Vin ÷ Roast Chicken

My Meat Sauce ÷ Proper Bolognese or Ragù

Beef Burgundy ÷ Ossobuco ÷ Braised Short Ribs

Brisket ÷ Meatloaf ÷ Pot Roast ÷ Beef Chili

Beef Tacos ÷ Pork Loin with Arugula Pesto

Sausages Braised with Turnips and Kale

Shepherd's Pie ÷ Halibut with Beurre Blanc

Pacific Spot Prawns with Green Sauce ÷ Simple Wild Salmon

Wild Salmon and Tzatziki ÷ Rainbow Trout with Spring Alliums

Pasta with the-Cheese-You-Have

Rob's Ricotta Pesto ÷ The Spaniard: A Sandwich

my latest poached chicken

Serves 4 to 6

I've poached so many chickens, and still I never tire of the moist, white meat. I do, however, tire of the dark meat, despite its virtues. It's full of good fats, unlike the mostly lean and admittedly blander breast meat. With one exception (cod liver oil), I don't eat or drink anything merely because it's good for you; I spent too many joyless, uninformed years doing that. What goes in my mouth has to please. Thus I have stubbornly avoided various food crazes (however reasonable) from bean sprouts and goat's milk to oat bran and green tea. But modest chicken, minimally dressed up with salt and olive oil, has held my attention despite its repeated appearance at the center of the plate. Whether you are new to chicken or not, I hope you'll consider My Latest Poached Chicken. When you're finished, you'll have a big, lovely piece of meat whose three main parts are all set for a good use. The best dark meat is ready for tonight's tortillas with brown rice, guacamole, and hot pepper sauce. Tomorrow, perhaps, you can make something gorgeous with the white meat, like a chicken salad or green Thai curry. Just don't strip the breast until the last minute, because lean meat dries out quickly. A gelatinous and meaty stock is already under way; it could be soup tonight, with or without meat—or you can freeze it for a rainy day. Here you will really notice the difference between a pastured chicken and the flabby indoor kind. The outdoor bird will be denser, in both culinary and nutritional terms, than its industrial counterpart. The pastured bird yields more flavor and minerals, and the reduced stock will be firm, like jelly, when it cools.

4-6 lb pastured chicken
2 carrots
2 onions
2 celery stalks
12 black peppercorns
1 thyme sprig
2 fresh bay leaves
olive oil

1. Rinse the chicken inside and out and let it drain.
2. Slice the carrots, onion, and celery.
3. Put the chicken, half of the vegetables, and half of the aromatics in a large pot and cover with cold water. Sometimes my pots are a bit small for a large chicken and the breast is peeking out of the water. Then I splash a little olive oil on the top of the bird and either baste it with the water or turn it so the top isn't dry or undercooked.
4. Simmer the chicken, uncovered, for 45 to 60 minutes. Skim off any foam.
5. When the chicken is thoroughly cooked (poke it with a skewer to see that the white meat is white, not pink), lift it out. Drain the chicken over a large bowl and save the liquid. Discard the spent aromatics and vegetables, which are now just soggy cellulose.
6. When the chicken is cool enough to handle, pull off the wings, legs, and thighs. Tear the best meat off the legs and thighs, but without being too thorough about it. (A bone broth with some meat is a luxury.) Separate the breast from the back, leaving the breast meat on the bones. Set aside the breasts and the stripped dark meat.
7. Put the back, wings, legs, and thigh bones in a fresh pot with the remaining fresh vegetables and aromatics.
8. Strain the poaching liquid, pour it over the bones, and simmer for at least 30 minutes and for up to 2 hours, adding more cold water if necessary.
9. Drain, cool, and put away the broth. ✛

thai chicken curry

Serves 6

This is a lovely dish, not my invention, with bottled condiments containing the not-so-secret Thai flavors, such as lemongrass and fermented fish, which make all the difference. Make it red, with a red pepper and red curry paste; or green, with the same items in that color. A simpatico seasonal vegetable is optional, but keep it simple; one is enough. Here's a great moment for one of my little luxuries. When I can't get to a farmers' market, I stop at the supermarket on the school run for organic bone-in, skin-on chicken breasts. Boy, are they delicious, and they cook fast. I roast them in 20 minutes. If you make this with cooked chicken, simply add the chicken with the basil.

2 onions

¼ c olive oil or 4 T coconut oil

1–2 T red or green Thai curry paste

2 red or green bell peppers

1 eggplant, 2 zucchini, 1 qt snow peas or ½ lb green beans

1 lb chicken meat

1 14-oz can of unsweetened coconut milk (not "light")

1 c fish or chicken stock

1 T fish sauce

1 knob of ginger

1 small bunch Thai basil

cooked rice to serve

1. Dice the onions and sauté them in the olive oil or coconut oil until half-soft. Add the curry paste and stir until fragrant, about 1 minute.

2. Cut the peppers and the other vegetable in shapes you like and pieces of even size. Add them to the onions and sauté until the vegetables soften.

3. While the vegetables are getting soft, chop or shred the chicken. Add it to the vegetables and sauté until it's lightly brown all over.

4. Add the coconut milk, stock, fish sauce, and a grating of ginger, and stir for 1 minute.

5. Chop or shred the basil. Add it to the pot and cook until the flavors have melded, about 5 minutes. Serve it over rice. ✚

white chicken stroganoff with dill

Serves 6

Here's a velvety cover for egg noodles or a dish on its own. Shallots are finer, milder, and sweeter than onions. Chardonnay leaves a nice residual sugar as it reduces. Something more dry—a typical sauvignon blanc—will leave more tang in the dish. Use more or less chicken stock, depending on how thick you like it, but please don't stint on the dill.

1 large chicken
2-3 shallots or 1 onion
1 large bunch of dill
3 cloves garlic
¼ c olive oil
½ c dry white wine
1 ½ c sour cream or crème fraîche
½-1 c chicken stock
salt and pepper

1. Poach the chicken (page 90). Drain it, reserving the stock. Reduce it further, by about half.
2. Shred the chicken meat.
3. Dice the shallots or slice the onion long and thin.
4. Chop the dill to yield a generous cup.
5. Mince the garlic or smash it in a garlic press.
6. Warm the olive oil in a large saucepan, add the shallots or onion and sauté them until they are half-soft.
7. Add the garlic.
8. Add the wine and reduce the liquid until most of it is gone.
9. Add the shredded chicken and the chopped dill, reserving a bit of dill for a garnish. Stir briefly to coat.
10. Add the sour cream or crème fraîche. Stir well and thin with chicken stock to taste.
11. Simmer for about 5 minutes and then let it stand.
12. Season and top with the reserved dill. ✣

thirteen ways of looking at a chicken

In his regular *New York Times* column, "The Minimalist," Mark Bittman wrote delicious recipes for unpretentious and omnivorous home cooks. Then he ventured into food and nutrition reporting, and along the way, Bittman decided that a substitute for chicken made of soybean protein had, at long last, met his standards. But the heart of his endorsement for this machine-made food was notably lukewarm. In a 2012 *New York Times* piece headlined "A Chicken Without Guilt," he wrote, "The thick strands that emerged on the other end didn't precisely resemble chicken strips, and when I tasted them unadulterated I found it bland, unexciting and not very chicken-like." Still, he cheered the novel food, calling it quite tasty once properly dressed. Pondering a reply to this departure from authentic minimalism, I thought of "Thirteen Ways of Looking at a Blackbird," by Wallace Stevens, and I wrote this homage to that great American poem for the real-food magazine *HandPicked Nation*.

I
Among twenty thousand chickens
The only moving things
Were forty thousand sad eyes.

II
I was of three minds
Are there only two ways of
Looking at a chicken?

III
Feathers flew in the great debate;
Omnivores and vegans cackled.
The mute chicken was a small part of the pantomime.
Does the chicken know what I know?

IV
On good farms, chickens scratch in dust, grass.
Muscles flex, bones grow dense.
The rooster protects his hens from hawks.
I eat these chickens.

V
Precious, pricey chicken! They say.
Privileged, pretentious people—
Not real Americans.

VI
Real Americans eat cheap, sad chicken.
Real Americans, rejoice!
Journalists declare the answer—
Hail "Chicken Without Guilt."

VII
Of course it is not chicken.
It is extruded soy protein.
It is water, canola, food coloring
And "chicken flavor."

VIII
It is proprietary;
You cannot watch it grow;
You cannot make it from scratch;
You cannot buy it at the farmers' market.

IX
It is coming to a fast-food joint near you.
Inches of editorial praise it first—faintly.
It is "not very chicken-like,"
But slathered with mayonnaise, it fools the pros,
    fools its fans!
Fans long to be fooled.

X
God—or Nature—made the chicken.
Man made the "Chicken Without Guilt."
It would not tempt a hungry fox,
Nor could it nourish a pregnant woman.

XI
Oh soy "chicken," where is thy skin?
How shall I make gribenes?
Oh soy "chicken," where are your bones?
Where shall I get broth, rich in minerals?
Oh soy "chicken," where is your fat?
Without Jewish penicillin, how to cure my
    husband's cold?

XII
They conjured fake breast milk from flour and water;
Babies died.
Mother's little helper, the TV dinner—
Family life withered.
And hydrogenated vegetable oil, dyed yellow?
Margarine kills, not butter.

XIII
"Chicken Without Guilt"
To hell with hunters and gatherers
To hell with omnivores and fire-builders
To hell with nutrition
To hell with pleasure
To hell with millennia of human culture
Guilt-free at last.

moist chicken with rice

Serves 4 to 6

You need more of this sort of dish: the no-recipe sort. It's a method, not a prescription, and I offer it in the spirit of spontaneous, paper-free cooking, the kind of cooking many resort to (I'll wager) on more nights than not. Rob always rummages the fridge for a spicy sauce or chutney, while I reach for the cayenne.

1 chicken
1 bay leaf
peppercorns
onions, cut in chunks
carrots, cut in chunks
olive oil
mushrooms, spinach, swiss chard
cooked brown rice

1. Poach (page 90) or roast (page 98) a whole chicken. Eat the best of it for one meal.
2. Strip the rest of the meat off the chicken, ideally in large pieces (lest they dry out), coat with a little olive oil, cover, and refrigerate.
3. Simmer the bones (and any meat you missed) in water with the bay leaf, a few peppercorns, 1 onion, perhaps 1 carrot, skimming the froth off the top, until the liquid is reduced by half—at least 1 hour.
4. Strain the stock and discard the bones and aromatics.
5. Slice the remaining onions thin. Cut the vegetables in pieces of equal size.
6. Heat the olive oil in a large, heavy skillet and sauté the onions until they are soft. Add the vegetables at the right time: thin carrot rounds before chopped spinach, for example.
7. Add the chicken, cutting the meat a little smaller if necessary, and the cooked rice to the hot onions and vegetables. Moisten with stock to taste and season. ✢

coq au vin

Serves 8

We wanted to honor our friend Paco at a grown-up dinner party. But it was two days before Christmas, and I was run ragged by months of interrupted sleep, twins who were still breast-feeding, and various deadlines. I figured I had a chance of pulling off a nice party without getting grouchy and still enjoying myself if I planned ahead, kept it simple, and (just this time) asked Michele Pulaski to cook the main dish: coq au vin, a classic braise I knew I'd love to make again and again, once I learned how. It's easy to make in advance and easy to serve. At a party, I don't like a finicky main dish, one that keeps me at the stove just as the talking gets going. So I did the Greenmarket shopping, delivered the pastured chicken to Michele, washed the greens, made the purée, and ordered the cake from Amy's Bread on Bleecker Street. We began our little party with St. Marcellin cheese, venison pâté, crackers, and Prosecco; then had a crisp Green Salad with Walnuts and Blue Cheese (page 50) and the coq au vin with root vegetables; finally there was chocolate cake heaped with whipped cream. Rob and I left on a high note, and our pillow talk was cheerful. I'd forgotten to add a little crème fraîche to the whipped cream, but I'm faithful to the first rule of hosting: never apologize for invisible errors.

½ lb thick-cut bacon

4 lb chicken, cut in 8 pieces, with the skin

½ lb pearl onions

6 cloves garlic

½ lb button mushrooms

2 c red wine (such as pinot noir or zinfandel)

2 c chicken stock

thyme

parsley

2 bay leaves

demi-glace (optional; page 56)

salt and pepper

1. Simmer the bacon in water for 1 to 2 minutes to remove some of the salt.
2. Dry the bacon, chop it, and brown it in a large pan. Remove the bacon.
3. In the same pan, brown the chicken. Remove the chicken.
4. In another pan, boil water and dip the pearl onions in it for less than a minute. When the onions are cool, peel them, leaving them whole.
5. Chop the garlic in large pieces.
6. Brown the onions in the chicken pan. Add the garlic and sauté briefly. Remove the onions and garlic.
7. Brown the mushrooms in the same pan. Remove the mushrooms.
8. Add the wine and scrape up all the browned bits with a wooden spoon. Reduce the wine for 2 or 3 minutes.
9. Add the chicken stock and simmer for 10 minutes.
10. Put the thyme and parsley in a bag or tie with a string.
11. Add the chicken, sautéed onions, herbs, and bay leaves to the pot. Cover and cook for about 30 minutes, or until the chicken is tender.
12. Uncover and reduce the liquid until it's just right. Remove the herbs and bay leaves. Here's the moment to add a few spoonfuls of (optional) demi-glace.
13. Add the sautéed mushrooms last, so they don't get spongy. Season and serve in shallow bowls on a bed of Root Vegetable Purée (page 159). ✛

roast chicken

When I opened my first farmers' market—and the first in London—in 1999, I had never roasted a chicken. It was the first meat recipe I learned to cook and my gateway to omnivory. After chicken came the harder stuff: bacon, beef, and so on. Perhaps I am not adventurous, but a nice roast chicken with a green salad is a Last Supper sort of meal for me. I like a large bird (five or six pounds), partly because it has lots of breast meat, but I often settle for smaller ones.

The best chickens are pastured, meaning they run free on grass and duck under shrubbery, eating leaves and bugs all the while. That's certainly nice for the chickens, but for the eater, they are noticeably superior to the flabby birds raised in large, dark, crowded barns. Expect more flavor and a firmer, less greasy, and more satisfying texture in a pastured bird. Exercise gives it stronger muscles and denser bones, both of which yield better stock. Air-chilling also makes a better chicken. Most chickens are cooled in a cold-water bath; it's quicker and cheaper but makes for watery meat.

Bigger birds are bound to get more popular. A pastured-chicken farmer told me that a large chicken makes better profits, because he can sell more meat on the same skeleton. The discerning eater also benefits from a mature bird, because it's a more dense creature in physiological terms, which means more flavor, protein, and minerals in the meat and bones—and, once again, superior stock. In my view, the stock is a primary consideration, not an afterthought.

Buy the best bird you can find and afford. I'm happy to spend good money on pastured chickens. However, I freely admit that we also buy commercial organic chickens that, I am certain, never ran free in the noonday sun or pecked a bug off a piece of chickweed. When you buy your first chicken, the nice farmer will ask you, "How big?" Don't worry about the weight; soon you will know how many mouths a chicken feeds in your house. When they are small, I buy two, or extra legs.

You'll also come to use your eye and experience to judge cooking times. There are rules of thumb (so many minutes per pound), but the variables—namely the chicken and your oven—are such that the rules aren't worth much. I studied them closely when I first tried roasting chickens, and no formula was as useful as cooking the next chicken proved to be. I've never had luck with a thermometer, but I love my skewer. Stick it deep in the thigh. If the juice runs clear, it's done—or nearly.

An hour or two before you turn on the oven, unwrap the bird, rinse it inside and out, and pat it dry. Set the oven to 350°F. Rub the chicken all over with olive oil, butter, or both. (In various side-by-side tests, all-butter was a clear winner.) Don't put oil or butter in the cavity; it just pools. Grind salt and pepper all over. A quartered onion, some rosemary, or half a lemon are nice aromatics inside. Sometimes I slip garlic slivers or herbs under the skin, but I find that garlic in the cavity lends a burnt flavor. I'm not too handy with flavorings, but I might mix ground spices (garam masala, ginger, cayenne pepper) with olive oil and then rub the oil over the bird an hour or two before cooking it.

The ultimate affordable, indestructible, and high-performing piece of kitchenware—a big iron skillet—is also my favorite pan for roasting chicken. When the oven is pretty hot, put the skillet in. When it reaches 350°F, take the skillet out, put the dressed bird in the hot skillet, and roast it. A three- or four-pound bird is ready in about forty-five minutes, a larger one in about an hour. Open the oven once to baste the skin with the fat from the pan and salt it one more time. Basting and salt are the secrets of golden, crispy skin. For basting, I do have a favorite gadget: a silicone brush. The bristles grab the fat, but they don't drop it until you paint the skin. Nor do they pull out, clump, frizz, or get smelly like natural bristles. Now I never spill hot fat, and cleanup is easy. If the skin isn't golden brown, your last move is to crank up the heat to 400°F for five minutes. Watch it like a hawk.

my meat sauce

Serves 4

Meat sauce isn't just about the meat. Mine is crammed with basil and zucchini in June, red peppers in September, diced carrots in February, and parsley year-round. I make it nearly once a week and do so with my eyes closed. A jar of ready-made sauce is a definite and welcome shortcut, and in New York and New Jersey, the Italian population means I'm spoiled for choice, but I still doctor it with my own meat or vegetables. One regrettable ingredient in jarred sauces is vegetable oil; at least one sauce made with olive oil, Lucini, is sold nationally. When you make your own sauce with canned tomatoes, leave time to reduce the liquid and deepen the flavors. Rob loves sauce with lots of garlic, which I undercook, and I love big chunks of ground beef rather than lots of bitty bits, so I don't pummel the beef too much in the browning. Lots of black pepper is good, and I finish with olive oil. When the sauce tastes too much of tomato, fresh cream or crème fraîche cuts the acidity. A day in the fridge does any red sauce a world of good. As for pasta, these days several brands of organic whole wheat pasta are quite satisfactory, and we sometimes indulge in the white flour version, too. Need I mention that we are extravagant with the grated Parmigiano-Reggiano or Pecorino Romano? Use a large heavy pot with a lid. I prefer cast iron coated with enamel.

2 onions
¼ c olive oil plus a little more
seasonal vegetables: red peppers, zucchini, yellow squash, or carrots
1-4 cloves garlic to taste
fresh basil (lots) or parsley (some) or oregano (a touch)
1 lb grass-fed ground beef
1 quart whole canned tomatoes, crushed canned tomatoes, or jarred sauce
salt and pepper
Parmigiano-Reggiano or Pecorino Romano to serve

1. Dice the onions. Heat the olive oil in a pot, add the onions, and sauté them gently until half-soft.
2. Meanwhile, dice the vegetables. Add them to the pot and cook, stirring, until all the vegetables are soft.
3. Cut the garlic in large chunks and chop the fresh herbs. I leave basil leaves larger and dice stronger ones, such as parsley or oregano. Careful: fresh oregano is powerful.
4. Add the garlic, herbs, and beef to the vegetables and sauté briefly, without breaking up the beef too much. Add more oil if necessary.
5. Mere minutes later, when the beef is brown and coated with the vegetable-flavored oil, add the tomatoes or jarred sauce and simmer over very low heat until the flavors join.
6. Add lots of fresh black pepper and salt to taste. (I'm careful with salt when using a jarred sauce, and I always account for the grating of salty cheeses to come.) ✛

proper bolognese or ragù

Italian meat sauces, or ragù, are typically made by sautéing vegetables and chopped meat, and then adding liquids such as wine or tomato sauce. This general method I learned from the exemplary, intimidating, and terribly useful *Sauces* by James Peterson. His recipes are classic, his instruction peerless. *Sauces* is an ideal gift for an uneducated former vegetarian recovering from a low-fat diet. I followed his instructions for the famous Bolognese sauce faithfully many times, and you can see from My Meat Sauce (page 100) how thoroughly I've taken up the method. In a few sentences I can explain how Peterson's authentic ragù differs from my more casual sauce. First, he begins the onion sauté with a good diced prosciutto. Second, he calls for three cups of tomato concassé with the liquid. To make concassé, blanch two pounds of tomatoes for about half a minute in boiling water. Peel the skin, remove the seeds, and dice the pulp. (If you don't peel and seed the tomatoes, you have simple "diced tomatoes," not concassé.) Separate the concassé into liquid and solids. Add the liquid part to the browned prosciutto, ground beef, and vegetables; simmer until the liquid has cooked away. Now add the diced pulp, cook for another 15 minutes, and, finally, add a cup of cream. Season, and you have real ragù.

beef burgundy

Serves 4 generously and 6 modestly

The cookbooks worth keeping have a voice, a point of view, a gestalt. I learned this bouef Bourguignon from *Les Halles Cookbook* by master narrator Anthony Bourdain. It's disgraceful that I haven't absorbed more recipes from the French bistro repertoire of Les Halles—one of the New York steak houses where I discovered how to eat red meat—but the beef Burgundy page is well splattered with trials, mostly involving different cuts of beef from different farms rather than other tinkering, because I know (just) enough not to muck about with Real Classics. In a couple of winters, I got it down, and now I have one winning beef stew. Many prefer to use chuck, a less expensive and somewhat chewier cut, and some recipes start with marinating chuck in red wine for a few hours or overnight. The alchemy lies in how a little beef, a little wine, and a lot of carrots make such a sweet, brown, silky sauce. The answer lies in the browning of the beef, the scraping of the pan, and in good stock or demi-glace. Bourdain calls for water and demi-glace, but I've had great luck with beef stock alone, and I think it's perfectly acceptable to use beef stock and demi-glace. I have even used a large scoop of gelatinous chicken broth. Beef Burgundy is much better the next day, and it looks good next to one of Rob's favorite sides: buttery Mashed Potatoes (page 156).

2 lbs top round or an oyster-cut London broil

8 medium onions

8 carrots

¼ c (or so) olive oil

2 T flour

1 c red burgundy

1 clove garlic

1 sprig rosemary or thyme

3-4 c beef stock or 3-4 c water plus 3-4 T demi-glace (page 56)

parsley to serve

1. Cut the beef into 1- to 2-inch cubes, trimming any gristly bits.
2. Slice the carrots in thin diagonals and the onions thin.
3. Put some of the olive oil in a large enamel stewing pot. Get it quite hot. Season the beef and brown it in batches in one layer only; if you overcrowd the pan, the beef won't color beautifully. Don't burn the olive oil. Set aside the beef.
4. Add some more olive oil to the hot, beefy pan. Add the onions and scrape up the caramelly bits with a wooden spoon. When the onions are half-soft, sprinkle the flour over them and stir some more. This can take 20 minutes.
5. When the onions are quite soft, add the wine. Keep scraping the bottom for every little treasure until the wine simmers.
6. Peel the garlic clove. Mince the herbs or put them in a small cloth bag.
7. Add the beef, carrots, garlic, herbs, and the stock or the water and demi-glace.
8. Cover and simmer for about 2 hours, or until the meat is falling-apart tender. Check it often. Do not let it stick to the bottom.
9. Remove the herbs and serve it with minced parsley. ✢

ossobuco

Serves 2

Ossobuco means "bone hole" in Italian. The center of the bone contains a treasure called marrow, which means silkiness and flavor. *Ossobuco* refers to both the marrow bone itself and to the stew, often tomato-based, made from it. The bone may come from veal, beef, or lamb. With good stock or demi-glace in the freezer, you can make this in darkest winter, when all you can scrounge up are carrots, potatoes, and onions. You'll need four cups of stock for braising, but it doesn't matter much what kind of stock. The genius of demi-glace is that it's reduced, but it's hard to say by just how much. A half-cup of good demi-glace is probably worth two cups of most beef stock. Just thin it with water. You will need a large, heavy, lidded pot that can go from stove to oven. Like most braises, this dish is better after resting for a day.

2 marrow bones 6-8 inches across
flour
salt and pepper
olive oil
2 onions
2 leeks
parsley
4 c chicken or beef stock or 1 c demi-glace (page 56)
2 c red wine
4 carrots
4 potatoes
salt and pepper

1. Set the oven to 300°F.
2. Dust the meat with flour and season.
3. Heat the olive oil in the Dutch oven. Brown the meat on all sides. Turn off the heat and remove the meat.
4. Chop the onions, leeks, and parsley.
5. In the same Dutch oven, soften the onions, leeks, and parsley, adding a little more olive oil or some stock if necessary as you scrape up the crispy bits with a wooden spoon.
6. When the vegetables are soft, add the browned meat, the rest of the stock, and the wine to the pot. If you like to eat the marrow (rather than letting it escape the bone and flavor the stew), set the bone with the large side of the opening facing up, like a horn.
7. Cover the pot and bake for 1 hour.
8. Meanwhile, chop the carrots and potatoes. After it has baked for 1 hour, add the vegetables and stir.
9. Bake for another hour. When it's falling-apart tender, season and serve. ✢

braised short ribs

Serves 4

It was May, and plucky little Jacob was recovering from minor surgery. When Rob brought home short ribs from the butcher, I could've clobbered him. On a hot day in a busy week, they were the last thing I wanted to learn how to cook or indeed eat.

But I was wrong. Yes, there are lots of steps here, and for the best effect you marinate them overnight, but each step is easy and the ribs are delicious. I'm glad I tried. Beef short ribs are larger and typically more tender and meaty than pork spare ribs. A slab of short ribs usually contains three or four ribs with a layer of boneless meat and fat. The most common cuts are "English," with the ribs separated and cut into two-inch lengths, and "flanken-style," with the ribs cut across the bone. I learned this basic method from meat master Tom Colicchio, a chef with a string of greenmarket-driven restaurants. I like ribs with soft polenta on the side.

6 short ribs with bones (about 4 lbs)

salt and pepper

¼ c olive oil

1 onion

2 carrots

3 celery stalks

2 cloves garlic

1 bottle dry red wine, perhaps a Cabernet Sauvignon

1 small bunch thyme

3 c beef stock

1. Rinse the ribs, pat dry, and season.
2. Heat the oil in a large Dutch oven and brown the meat well, turning each piece once. Set the ribs in a bowl.
3. Chop the onions, carrot, celery, and garlic.
4. Add the vegetables (and more oil if necessary) to the meat pan and brown until soft, about 20 minutes.
5. Add the wine and thyme and bring to a boil.
6. Pour the hot marinade over the ribs and let it cool.
7. Cover and refrigerate overnight, turning the ribs once.
8. Set the oven to 350°F.
9. Put the meat and the marinade in a Dutch oven. Add the stock and bring it to a boil.
10. Cover the pot and bake the ribs for about 90 minutes, until the meat is just tender.
11. Remove the lid and bake for about 45 more minutes. Turn the meat once or twice. The ribs are ready when the sauce is reduced by half and the meat is very tender. For a silkier effect, remove the meat and strain the sauce. (If the sauce seems too greasy, chill it until the fat hardens, skim the fat, and reheat.) ✢

brisket

Serves 6 to 8

The *cut* known as brisket comes from the breast or lower chest of beef or veal. It's full of flavor, and it's also full of collagen, which requires some attention to be tender in the eating. The cook has several options. One is liquid; water helps turn collagen into delicious, delicate gelatin. Another is long, slow cooking. A third is leaving the fat cap on, the better to protect the meat from drying out. Thus Texas barbecue calls for a long marinade followed by slow cooking over indirect heat, with lots of smoke. The *dish* known as brisket is simply Jewish pot roast. It became apparent that I would have to learn how to make a good one. At first I avoided this; then I made some lousy briskets; and finally I asked Michele Pulaski, who cooked for our wedding and has made briskets for many Seders, to show me how. Her secret is good demi-glace. Michele says you can make the brisket two or three days before you eat it, but I've never managed such advance planning. I do know that the leftovers are good, because I have seen Rob very happy with a brisket sandwich.

5-6 lb brisket
salt and pepper
½ c olive oil
2 carrots
4 onions
2 celery stalks
2 c demi-glace (page 56)
2 c red wine, perhaps a Burgundy
1 6-oz can or tube tomato paste

1. Set the oven to 350°F.
2. Cut the meat in half. Rinse it and pat it dry. Season generously.
3. Heat the olive oil in a large heavy pan that can go from stove to oven, and brown the meat on all sides. (Searing seals the fat cap to preserve the juices.) Set aside the meat.
4. Cut the carrots, two of the onions, and the celery in chunks and put them in the same pan. Add the demi-glace and wine. Bring to a simmer and reduce for as long as it takes to scrape up all the good bits with a wooden spoon.
5. Smear the meat all over with tomato paste.
6. Set the meat gently into the vegetables and liquid. Cover with foil or the lid. Bake for about 1 hour.
7. Cut the remaining two onions into very thin pieces. After 1 hour, uncover the meat and put the onion slices right on it—not in the liquid. They will stick to the tomato paste and stay there, browning.
8. Bake for another hour or so. The meat is ready when it pulls away in shreds. Let it cool.
9. Remove the meat. Put the meat and the broth in separate containers and refrigerate.
10. When the sauce cools, remove any risen fat.
11. Warm, simmer, strain, and reduce the sauce by about one-third. Season.
12. When you are ready to serve the brisket, slice it *cold*. Reheat the meat in the sauce. ✢

meatloaf

Serves 6

Here's another supper to make by heart—or, if you're Emily Duff, with beef heart. My real-food friend grinds organ meats for her meatloaf—brilliant frugal traditional food, the kind I aspire to. Meanwhile, here's my daily loaf of meat. A mix of beef and pork is best, I think. If you use beef alone, meatloaf is too like a square burger. Two pounds of meat generously fills my standard glass loaf pan and definitely requires two eggs, two slices of toast, and a full hour in the oven. One pound of meat, one egg, and one piece of toast, on the other hand, makes a perfectly nice loaf in 35 to 40 minutes. Having tried diced spinach, zucchini, fennel, and other seasonal vegetables, I always return to the usual suspects: carrots, celery, onions, leeks. Dice them small. Instead of ketchup, try the best tomato jam in New York. Made by Katchkie Farm with an ingenious formula involving organic tomatoes, onions, cider vinegar, garlic, cayenne, cloves, allspice, and ginger, it ought to be the industry standard. You can see why it goes with meatloaf. Ketchup at the bottom of the pan turns silky, while ketchup on top becomes crispy and sweet. I don't grudge the children extra ketchup on the plate, either. We like Sir Kensington's, a self-mocking, retro-vintage brand that's beautifully spiced and not too sweet.

1 onion
1 small bunch parsley or sage
1 carrot
1 celery stalk (optional)
⅓ c olive oil
salt and pepper
2 slices bread
1 lb ground beef
1 lb ground pork
2 eggs
Katchkie Farm tomato jam or fine ketchup

1. Set the oven to 350°F.
2. Dice the onion, herbs, carrot, and (optional) celery.
3. In a large pan, heat the olive oil and sauté the vegetables until soft. Season with salt and pepper.
4. Toast the bread, let it get completely cool to dry out, and make bread crumbs. (I use the food processor.)
5. Add the beef, pork, eggs, and bread crumbs to the vegetables and stir well.
6. Coat the bottom of a loaf-shaped glass dish with tomato jam, and pack the mixture firmly in the dish. Spread a little more jam on top.
7. Bake for about 1 hour, until it's bubbling. Sometimes I drain off some fat and juice, and sometimes I don't. Let it cool a bit before serving. ✛

pot roast

Serves 8

French cooks soak the beef in red wine. German speakers soak it in buttermilk. Both methods produce a tender and tasty forkful of meat. Be generous with the olive oil. "Light" recipes calling for a teaspoon of oil make it impossible to brown the meat or soften the onions properly. I've watched many professional cooks brown the meat, and they really smoke it. But I don't care for burned fat splattering my stove and hair. I brown it well, without making a mess, but I cannot promise that my results are identical. The inimitable and indispensable flavors of seared meat and browned onions derive from a famous bit of kitchen chemistry known as the Maillard reaction. When amino acids (in meat) and a reducing sugar (usually provided by wine or vegetables) are heated, multiple reactions occur, producing an array of volatile compounds responsible for flavor. In short, browning is chemically complex but easy to do. The optional beef shanks add an extra layer of flavor without any extra work. It's worth the extra planning to marinate the meat and to serve pot roast the day after you make it. In our house it makes a great welcome-home dish when Rob has been traveling. For a dressier version, strain the sauce and discard the vegetables.

1 bottle red wine, perhaps a Burgundy
3 lbs bottom round or boneless chuck
2 bone-in beef shanks (optional)
¼ c olive oil
salt and pepper
2 large onions
4 carrots
2 cloves garlic
1 bay leaf
a few sprigs of thyme
1 qt beef stock or 1 qt water plus 1 c demi-glace (page 56)

1. Set aside 1 cup of the wine. Cover the meat with the rest of the wine and marinate for 2 hours on the counter or overnight in the fridge.
2. Set the oven to 325°F.
3. Pat the meat very dry and season generously.
4. Heat some of the olive oil and brown the meat in a large, oven-ready pot with a lid. Remove the meat and set it aside.
5. Slice the onions and put them in the meat pan. Add more olive oil and sauté until they are completely soft and brown on the edges; spend at least 20 minutes on the onions—a prime example of the Maillard reaction at work. With a wooden spoon, scrape all the brown bits off the bottom. If they're stubborn, a splash of wine will smooth the way.
6. Peel and chop the carrots and garlic. Add the meat, carrots, garlic, and aromatics (in a cloth bag if you like) to the onions. Cover the meat with the reserved cup of wine and the stock or demi-glace and water.
7. Put the lid on the pot and put it in the oven. Gently poke the pot roast from time to time, and add more beef stock if necessary. In 1 to 2 hours, the meat will be falling-apart tender. ✛

beef chili

Serves 6 to 8

I call this "green" chili, and it's one of two occasions when I prefer a green to a red bell pepper. The other is Italian sausages with griddled peppers and onions. For "red" chili, I use a red bell pepper. I drop some chocolate in for a molé feel.

1 dried ancho pepper
1 onion
1 green (or red) bell pepper
1 slice bacon (optional)
¼ c olive oil
2 cloves garlic
1 tsp cinnamon
10 cumin seeds or ½ tsp ground cumin
1 tsp chili powder
2 lbs ground beef
1 qt (28-oz can) crushed tomatoes
1 tsp cider vinegar
1 c beer or beef stock (optional)
2 squares 70% chocolate or 2 tsp cocoa powder (optional)
salt and pepper
sour cream to garnish
jack cheese to garnish
parsley to garnish

1. Soak the ancho in hot water for about 5 minutes. When it's soft, dice it to yield about 1 teaspoon.
2. Dice the onions, bell pepper, and (optional) bacon, and sauté them in the olive oil.
3. While the onions are getting soft, dice the garlic. When the onions are half-done, add the garlic, ancho, cinnamon, cumin, and chili powder and cook for a few minutes, being careful not to burn the spices.
4. Add the ground beef and sauté until it's light brown.
5. Add the tomatoes, the vinegar, and the (optional) beer or stock and chocolate. Stir and simmer until it has cooked down and the flavors are melded, about 20 minutes. Let it rest overnight if you have time.
6. Serve hot with sour cream, grated jack cheese, and minced parsley. ✢

beef tacos

Serves 6

Boneless chuck is a tasty and affordable piece of meat, and tacos make a crowd-pleasing dinner. It's hard to find a good adobo paste, so you could substitute ground adobo seasoning from Frontier or Simply Organic and mix it with a spoonful of olive oil. The meat is easily made one day ahead and will taste delicious after sitting; the rest is mere assemblage. Serve with flour or corn tortillas, shredded lettuce, Griddled Onions (page 139), diced tomatoes, guacamole, and sour cream.

3 lbs boneless chuck, boneless short ribs, or bottom round
1 onion
1 beer, dark or light
1 c water
½ c demi-glace (page 56) or 1 c beef stock
1 T cider vinegar
pinch of cinnamon
1 tsp chili powder
1 dab adobo sauce or 1 tsp ground adobo seasoning
salt and pepper

1. Cut the beef into strips 3 inches long, trimming any gristly bits.
2. Slice the onion in thin pieces.
3. Put the meat, sliced onion, beer, 1 cup of water, and the demi-glace or stock in a heavy pan and simmer over medium heat. The meat will not quite be covered with liquid.
4. Simmer for about 1 hour. Add a little more beer or water if it gets too dry. Still, the liquid should not fully cover the meat.
5. When you can pull the meat apart in long shreds, add the vinegar and spices. Cook for a few more minutes. Season.
6. If you are making the tacos now, pull the meat apart right in the pan, using two forks.
7. If you are serving the tacos tomorrow, let the meat rest in the fridge unshredded. ✤

pork loin with arugula pesto

Serves 6

A boneless, rolled pork loin is not a cut to buy often. If you buy pastured pork, it's pricey, and there is more moisture and flavor elsewhere on a pig—near bones, for example. That said, it's tender and mild, it can be elegant, and it's very easy to cook. This recipe is an easy way to make it more assertive. It slices nicely if you tie it up tightly, and you can serve it hot or cold. Do not hesitate to make more of the lemony pesto. You'll want to slather more on the meat at the table.

½ c pine nuts
1 lemon
½ lb arugula
2 cloves garlic
½ tsp unrefined sea salt
¼ c olive oil
3 lb rolled pork loin
salt and pepper
string to tie up the pork

1. Set the oven to 350°F.
2. In a dry pan, toast the pine nuts briefly over very low heat, shaking or stirring them often; do not let them burn.
3. Juice the lemon.
4. Put all the ingredients except the pork in a food processor and pulse until the sauce is evenly chunky. Set aside a little pesto for serving.
5. Unroll the pork and season it all over. Smear the inside with most of the pesto, roll it up tightly, and tie it with string.
6. Roast the pork for 20 minutes or until it's pink through.
7. Slice it gently and serve with more pesto. ✛

sausages braised with turnips and kale

Serves 6

Here's a dish you can make in October, when fall greens are just appearing, or in April, when overwintered greens are staging a comeback. Meanwhile, don't feel locked in by the vegetables below. Try butternut squash or kohlrabi in place of the turnips, add thin fennel to the onions, or toss in a handful of raisins. Use a wide, shallow pan. My enameled, cast-iron pan is more than a foot across and just three inches deep. You'll need another skillet to make the mushrooms come out right. In the instructions, I've been fussy about the order in which you add the vegetables. No apologies: properly cooked plants are a personal obsession. But your job, of course, is to eyeball it. You could also use a little cider in place of the chicken stock.

1 onion

2 yellow or purple-top turnips

2 cloves garlic

3 bunches (about 1 lb) of Red Russian kale, Green Wave mustard, or Tuscan kale

1 lb mushrooms (Portobello, Shitake, Crimini)

2 lbs sweet Italian sausage

¼-½ c olive oil

1-2 c chicken stock

pinch of cayenne

1 nutmeg

chunky sea salt, such as Maldon or Jacobsen

salt and pepper

1. Slice the onions thin, dice the turnips, and chop the garlic. Chop the greens stems in small pieces and the leaves in larger ones; keep the stems and leaves separate.
2. Cut the sausages in 2-inch slices on the diagonal, heat some olive oil in a large braising pan, and brown the sausages on both sides. Remove the meat and set it aside.
3. Sauté the onions in the same pan, with a little more olive oil, until they are half-soft.
4. Add the turnips and garlic and cook until the turnips are just short of tender.
5. Add the stems of the greens and soften somewhat. Then add the leaves and wilt them.
6. Add the sausages, stock, cayenne, and a grating of nutmeg to the vegetables. Cover and simmer over low heat.
7. Brush or pat the mushrooms clean—do not wash—and slice them in even pieces, no stems. In another skillet, heat a little fresh olive oil. Put the mushrooms in the pan in one layer, sprinkle with the salt, and let them color before turning. Set the mushrooms on a paper towel and do the next batch.
8. When the flavors have melded and the vegetables are perfectly tender, season, top with the hot mushrooms, and serve. ✚

shepherd's pie

Serves 8

A baked meat casserole with a mashed potato crust, "cottage" pie is genuine peasant food. This old-timey dish, which has been made more or less like this from leftover roast meat for a good three hundred years, is brand-new to my repertoire, and I owe it all to Rob, for whom I make lamb at Passover, and to Michele Pulaski, who showed me the way of the lamb *and* the shepherd's pie. If you don't have leftover lamb, start with freshly ground lamb or beef, and brown it with a diced onion in plenty of olive oil. If, like me, you don't use up the tomato paste in the can and it goes to waste, buy one of those good tubes and keep it in the fridge.

2 ½ lbs Yukon gold or other good mashing potatoes
2–3 c milk
¼ c (½ stick or 2 oz or 4 T) butter, plus more for topping
unrefined sea salt
leftover leg of lamb yielding 1 lb of meat or
1 lb ground lamb or beef
2 onions
1 carrot
3 T demi-glace (page 56)
1 T tomato paste
1 sprig rosemary
1 nutmeg
¼ c olive oil
1 lb frozen green peas

1. First make the mashed potatoes: Boil salted water. Peel, chop, and boil the potatoes until they're soft. Mash by hand with the milk and butter. Season.
2. Strip the leftover leg of lamb, put the meat in a pan, and cover it with cold water.
3. Peel and quarter 1 onion. Slice the carrot. Add the onion, the carrot, the demi-glace, the tomato paste, the rosemary, and a grating of nutmeg to the meat.
4. Simmer until all the liquid is cooked down.
5. Pick over the meat. Remove the carrot, rosemary twig, and any cartilage that may have snuck in. Shred the large pieces of meat. You can do all this one day ahead.
6. When you're ready to assemble the dish, set the oven to 350°F.
7. Dice the second onion and sauté in olive oil until very soft. Drop the frozen peas in and cook them for one minute.
8. Layer the ingredients in a large (9-by-13-inch) baking dish with the lamb on the bottom, the peas in the middle, and the mash on top. Dot the top with butter and bake for 20 to 30 minutes. If the meat and mashed potatoes are cold, it will take longer. It's ready when the mashed potato peaks are brown. You can also broil it for a minute or two to get the brown peaks. ✛

halibut with beurre blanc

Makes 2 cups, enough to dress 8 servings of fish

My fish and seafood shopping is bicoastal. From my local greenmarkets, I buy mostly fish from small and family-owned boats bringing brine-fresh Long Island catch. My local favorites include oily bluefish, carmine tuna steaks, and scallops so fresh I eat them raw with olive oil and a squeeze of orange. I also buy frozen fish from West Coast purveyors of wild Alaskan catch. From Pacific waters, I like salmon, halibut, and spot prawns. The high standards of these fishmongers ensure that my fish is frozen when very fresh; it arrives in sparkling condition. Such gorgeous fish needs little enhancement, but I wanted to learn something more elegant, so I turned to James Peterson's *Sauces* to learn beurre blanc, the traditional sauce of the Loire Valley, a land where butter reigns. Butter contains lecithin, which will emulsify (or bind) the fat and the acid to make a stable sauce. The crispy acidity of muscadet makes it the traditional wine to balance the richness of the butter, but variations are yours to devise. Try a heavier wine with more residual sugar, like chardonnay; rice wine vinegar for an Asian flavor; or lemon juice. I like salmon, halibut, and scallops with beurre blanc. This classic pairing is also nutritious: the saturated fats in butter help the body absorb the omega-3 fatty acids in the fish.

4 shallots
½ c white wine
½ c white wine vinegar
4 T cream
2 c (4 sticks or 1 lb) cold unsalted butter
unrefined sea salt
8 pieces salmon or halibut or 2 lbs scallops
parsley

1. Mince the shallots.
2. Put the shallots, wine, and vinegar in a saucepan and simmer until almost all the liquid is gone. Do not allow the shallots to brown.
3. Add the cream.
4. Cut the butter into cubes and add to the pan. Whisk continuously over high heat until all the butter has melted.
5. Adjust the sauce as needed. A "flat" sauce may need a few drops of wine vinegar; if it is too sharp, add more butter.
6. Season with salt. Fine chefs strain out the shallots.
7. Season the fish with salt and sauté in a little olive oil or butter. Turn it once, let the other side color, and serve it immediately with beurre blanc and minced parsley. ✢

pacific spot prawns with green sauce

Serves 4 to 6

Modern aquaculture is disheartening. Shrimp farms destroy miles of delicate coastal ecologies, especially mangrove swamps, only to move on to the next virgin territory. Farmers treat the pools with antibiotics to prevent disease and with pesticides to kill bugs. Once I despaired about the shrimp on my plate. Then I discovered wild Pacific spot prawns. These juicy, springy, and briny things will show you at once that farmed shrimp are watery, flabby, and fishy. Spot shrimp are abundant in the clean, cold waters of British Columbia. Mine arrive frozen in a block of brine, shells and tails still on, from Vital Choice. I think of spot shrimp as tiny lobsters—an extravagance, to be sure, and one I enjoy fully. Whether you sauté, stew, or grill the prawns, cook them in the shell. Eating will be a bit messy, but the richer flavor is your reward. Instruct your guests to save the shells, which you will boil briefly. Reduce the liquid and freeze it. Now you'll have a splash of shrimp stock for the next batch of prawns. Many pairings suit this dish: garlic and chili flakes, lemon and parsley, shallots and tarragon. Serve with bread to mop up the juices.

15-20 large prawns (a 12-oz tub)
1 small bunch cilantro
¼ c olive oil
2 cloves garlic
1 small bunch Thai basil
2 T butter
splash of white wine or fish broth (optional)
unrefined sea salt
1 lime
cilantro to garnish

1. If you're using frozen prawns, defrost them on the counter and save the brine for stock. If there's still ice clinging to the prawns, I rinse them, but only when pressed for time, because it's a shame to waste the brine. Pat the shrimp dry.

2. Following the curving spine of the prawn, cut a slit in the shell. This lets the fats and flavors meet the flesh, and it makes it easier to peel them at the table.

3. Remove the thick stems from the cilantro and set aside a little for the garnish. Put the rest of the cilantro leaves in the food processor with the olive oil, garlic, and basil. Make a quick, rough pesto.

4. Heat the butter in a large skillet.

5. Toss the shrimp into the hot butter. Let them turn coral on one side and then flip them.

6. Add the (optional) wine or fish stock and cook it off, tossing the shrimp around, for a moment or two.

7. Add the pesto and toss again. The prawns are ready when the butter, pesto, and juices have all merged nicely. All this takes just a few minutes.

8. Serve with a grind of salt, a squeeze of lime, and a scattering of the reserved cilantro leaves. ✛

simple wild salmon

Serves 6 to 8

Buy salmon wild from cold, clear Pacific waters. It's leaner, firmer, and cleaner than the flabby, farmed sort sometimes labeled "Atlantic." It will also be free of the antibiotics and pesticides fish farms use to fight fish lice. Salmon farms are hostile to wild salmon; they kill off nearby wild cousins, including Atlantic, steelhead, pink, chum, and coho salmon. Since Alaska banned salmon farming, its wild salmon fisheries have thrived. If you live near those waters, rejoice and buy fresh wild salmon. On the East Coast, my best salmon choice is usually frozen. The ruby fish, rich in omega-3 fats and colorful antioxidants, stays very fresh in my trusty freezer. A whole side of salmon serves six to eight. However you cook it, let it be pale pink on the outside and a moist, rosy pink in the middle. Serve with crème fraîche or butter, beurre blanc (page 115), or sauce gribiche (page 36).

Baking

Set the oven to 350°F. Wrap the fish in foil or parchment paper. Dress it lightly with olive oil or dot it with butter. Add a splash of white wine; rosemary, thyme, or a bay leaf; perhaps a slice of lemon. Season all over. Seal up the package and bake it for about 20 minutes.

Poaching

The best poaching liquid is fish stock (page 57) or, as I was surprised to learn from Michele Pulaski, chicken stock (page 55). Water is a little . . . watery. If you must poach in water, add a bit of white wine and olive oil. Put the salmon in a large, flat pan, and cover it with the liquid. Add a bay leaf, a couple of peppercorns, and a grind of salt. Simmer uncovered for 10 to 12 minutes.

wild salmon with tzatziki

Tzatziki is a Greek and Turkish *meze* (appetizer or snack), made of strained yogurt, cucumbers, and garlic. It's served cold with fish, vegetables, and meat and makes a great dip for pita chips. Straining the yogurt results in a dense sauce with a more intense flavor. Sheep milk yogurt would be nice here, and traditional. The salmon you can bake or poach in your own way, one day ahead if you like. Though nothing goes better with salmon than butter, for this dish, I would use olive oil if I were baking the fish, because it's Mediterranean and summery. Use a tender Persian cucumber; if the skins are very thin, there's no need to peel them. (See further notes on cucumbers on page 10.) You can make both the fish and the tzatziki one day ahead (photo on page 88).

2 c yogurt
1 clove garlic
1 T olive oil
1 lemon
1 small bunch mint
1 small bunch dill
3 cucumbers
salt and pepper
1 whole side of wild salmon, baked or poached (page 118)

1. Set a clean cloth in a strainer over a bowl. Drain the yogurt for at least 1 hour or overnight in the fridge.
2. Crush and chop the garlic and cover it with the olive oil to rest awhile.
3. Zest the lemon. Juice it to yield about 1 tablespoon.
4. Save a little dill for a garnish. Chop the rest of the mint and the dill to yield about 3 tablespoons of each.
5. Shred one cucumber on the largest grater hole.
6. Mix all the ingredients, season, and refrigerate.
7. When it's time to serve the salmon, slice the other cucumbers in very thin coins. Set the fish on a serving platter and place the cucumber slices on it so that they overlap and cover the fish like scales.
8. Put the cold tzatziki in a serving bowl and scatter a little dill on top. Serve it with the fish. ✢

rainbow trout with spring alliums

Serves 2

Rainbow trout is a farmed fish you can eat year-round and with impunity, ecologically speaking. It's a true trout raised in clean, cold-water pools by many farmers in my region. I can't resist these delicate pink fish, which I associate with spring alliums, young beets, greens of all kinds, and a shaving of ginger. I call for fresh (uncured) garlic because I like to enjoy it during its short season. In July, farmers pull mature garlic and let it dry. Once dry (cured), the garlic stores well, and you can buy it at the markets all winter. So the moment to find fresh garlic, which is moist and mild, is in June. New potatoes or any spring green would make a nice side dish here. I also love a smoked rainbow trout with a spoonful of crème fraîche laced with fresh horseradish. Take the same trio of smoked fish, crème fraîche, and horseradish, mash it up with a fork, and spread it on oat crackers. Brook trout, another tasty freshwater fish, is actually a cousin of arctic char.

8 young scallion bulbs

4 young leeks

3-4 cloves garlic

¼ c olive oil

1 knob of fresh ginger

1 whole fresh rainbow trout, gutted

salt and pepper

1. Set the oven to 350°F.
2. Clean and split the scallions and leeks. Cut the leeks in thin strips. Chop the garlic.
3. Heat the olive oil in an iron skillet and sauté the scallions and leeks until they are colored on all sides.
4. Add the garlic, toss it all together, and cook another minute.
5. Give it a quick grating of fresh ginger.
6. Rinse the trout, pat it dry, and season all over.
7. Put the vegetables in a piece of parchment paper or foil. Stuff a few greens in the trout and bury it on all sides. Fold or staple up the packet.
8. Bake for about 10 minutes and serve at once. ✛

pasta with the-cheese-you-have

Serves 4

On a hot and humid afternoon at the playground, Julian (then three) had been a little sick to his stomach, so when he asked for spaghetti, I was not inclined to say no and give him beef, as planned. Let the boy fill up on coconut water, oranges, and pasta if he was hungry at all. So I gladly made him Pasta with the-Cheese-We-Had, one of my staples. We had Mimolette and Mary Quicke's clothbound cheddar, both decent melting cheeses, on hand. One was yellow and one white, like bicolor corn. Alas, even this friendly plan was derailed by the fickle tastes of a sick child. Julian called for spaghetti with olive oil, which he got, while his father ate the bowl of cheesy deliciousness—a real slice of my real-food life. DeLallo is a consistently good organic Italian whole wheat pasta, and there are many others.

1 lb whole wheat pasta
3 T unsalted butter
1 c the-cheese-you-have
½–1 c whole milk
black pepper

1. Boil pasta in plenty of salted water. I prefer it well-cooked to al dente.
2. Drain the pasta, put it back in the pan, and butter it generously.
3. Grate a fist-sized pile of melting cheeses.
4. While the pasta is still hot, and perhaps with the heat on very low, mix the cheese and pasta until the cheese melts.
5. Slowly add a little milk and stir well until the sauce is smooth.
6. Serve at once with plenty of black pepper. ✢

rob's ricotta pesto

Serves 4

I love cold herb sauces of all kinds. Rob's ricotta pesto is mild, smooth, creamy, summery, and, like any pesto, easy.

2 c loosely packed basil leaves
2 cloves garlic
½ c ricotta
½ c olive oil
½ c Parmigiano-Reggiano
salt and pepper
1 lb pasta

1. Boil lots of salted water for the pasta you prefer.
2. Put all the ingredients in the food processor and whiz until very smooth.
3. Taste and season.
4. Cook and drain the pasta, leaving it a little moist, and toss it with the pesto while it's still warm. Serve at once. ✛

the spaniard: a sandwich

Rob Kaufelt

I had to outsource a sandwich recipe. Here's my husband, Rob, a grocer for forty years, a man of distinct and highly reliable taste, the owner of Murray's Cheese, and a born short-order cook—his other specialty is late-morning egg dishes—on how he goes about making a sandwich. He's the master of the fridge rummage, and I feel good knowing that the ingredients he finds there, such as my Griddled Onions (page 139), take any sandwich up a level. The Spaniard, one of the many changing melts made fresh on the spot at Rob's Greenwich Village shop, holds American Surryano ham, young Manchego, silky membrillo, and griddled red peppers and onions on toasted Sullivan Street Bakery Pullman. —NP

Nina's assignment—tell them how to make a sandwich—seemed too simple, akin to showing a man how to put on his belt. But on second thought, there is an art to putting flavors on a platform of bread, and it's an art I enjoy. Certainly sandwiches have earned me an unrivaled place in the kitchen. Nina freely admits she can't make a good sandwich, and I can't do without one.

First, the perusal of the fridge and its contents: the cheese, meats, vegetables, condiments. Already the options are many, and let's not forget the bread. Any bread in our house will do, though its condition may demand toasting.

Although the towering Dagwood of my youth is ever-appealing, in maturity I strive for simplicity: a good mountain cheese, perhaps a cave-aged Gruyère, is ideal; a slice of great meat, preferably pork (I'm partial to Serrano ham, domestic and foreign); Nina's shriveled onions and peppers, which are at once sweet and savory; and a spicy condiment, perhaps a good mustard. I'm a cheesemonger, of course, so grilling the whole stack in a pan of butter is always tempting, the results oozy, gooey, salty, spicy, crunchy, buttery.

Now a pickle, if one is to be found. (Daily we hear of a new Brooklyn pickle company.)

Slice it in half, plate it, and the lads will come begging for a bite, with nimble Rose hot on their trail; they know their mother is not the house sandwich-master. Three cheers for great bread and the leftover refrigerator bits crammed between.

perfect sides

My Way with Vegetables

Griddled Red Peppers ÷ Griddled Onions

Green Bean Salad with Options

Asparagus with Eggs ÷ Asparagus with Hollandaise Sauce

Smashed and Braised New Potatoes

Broccoli with Cheese Sauce ÷ Cauliflower Fried in Parmigiano

Ratatouille ÷ Roasted Beets with Blue Cheese and Walnuts

Mashed Potatoes ÷ Roasted Sweet Potatoes ÷ Rebbie's Root Gratin

Root Vegetable Purée ÷ Sweet Onion Custard

An Approach to Brown Rice ÷ Quinoa

Quinoa with Roasted Vegetables

my way with vegetables

Plant a radish.
Get a radish.
Never any doubt.
That's why I love vegetables;
You know what you're about!
  —The Fantasticks

Most of my farm memories are of abundance. The basement fridge was filled with asparagus in spring and eggs all year. From June to September the cool basement held zucchini, yellow squash, and cucumbers. In August the greenhouses shaded hundreds of baskets of heirloom and hybrid tomatoes. We picked wagons of corn every morning, bushels of beans every afternoon, trailer-loads of watermelons weekly. Lettuce ran for miles under white row covers. We picked blueberries for market only once a week; it's much easier to be sure they are fully ripe if you leave them alone. But in between these official blueberry market picks there were thousands of ripe blueberries for "home use." In the pick-your-own strawberry days, we grew so many strawberries that the cars of Saturday and Sunday pickers filled our driveway and spilled over on the grass. In the fall, onions and garlic drying on pallets covered the barn floor. We filled the green flatbed Ford with pumpkins and winter squash.

I also remember the way the wire handles on the bushel baskets cut into your hands when you lifted fifty pounds of Gold Star melons and the foggy feeling when the alarm rang at four in the morning to go to market. I remember how my feet sank into the muck when I washed my hair in the pond, bloodsuckers constantly on my mind. And I remember, too, the joy of jumping in the pond after long mornings spent mulching tomatoes with prickly straw, how warm blueberries taste, making raw-milk coffee smoothies after school with my brother, and the signs my mother would leave on the kitchen table, lest we forget our duties: CHARLES AND NINA COME TO BARNYARD BEANS 3:45.

But those sensations, pleasant and less-so, pale next to the equally tactile memories of plenty, and plenty is the reason I cook and eat vegetables the way I do. If there is one thing I miss about farm life—and there are many—it is, bluntly, the free vegetables. They lie there colorfully, quietly, amply. They ripen and rot inexorably. Their fate is binary: they will be cooked or composted. One or the other, it doesn't matter which. Man, woman, child; cow, cucumber, or compost; we have one thing in

common. Each is nothing more than a temporary, complex arrangement of carbon molecules. And nothing less.

The farm was many years behind me when Brian Halweil, the editor of *Edible East End*, introduced me to the Italian word *scorpacciata*, meaning "to eat copious amounts of a certain food in its peak local season." Here was a single word for the essence of the life we had led. The idea is that you are lucky to be swimming in, say, garlic scapes and that this pleasure is all the more precious for being fleeting.

So my attitudes toward vegetables in the kitchen—attitudes that I urge you to adopt without the intervening, time-consuming farm experience—were sown in the fields of Loudoun County, Virginia. But I have always felt that my homegrown gratitude was anointed by this beautiful word and all the Italian meals it has inspired.

If you want to live more like a farm girl and closer to vegetables, this is my advice. First, you must buy vegetables, and you must buy them every few days, and you must buy a lot of them. If there are no vegetables in the fridge, you are not eating vegetables. My friend John objects, "The trouble with vegetables is that they are always rotting in my fridge and I'm always throwing them away."

So are mine. As long as vegetables are part of the great carbon cycle, waste doesn't bother me too much, though I feel wretched when I'm not able to compost the rotters and the trimmings. Thus I always buy and make vast quantities. I've never bought or cut up or cooked a lone zucchini, always two pounds or more. When some nice thing or another is beginning to turn, I pounce. I roast all the peppers, griddle all the spring onions, boil all the corn at once.

Another self-evident maxim—which you may have overlooked, but which did not escape the notice of Clarence Birdseye, father of the flash-frozen pea: you will eat more vegetables when they are already prepared. I love room-temperature leftovers and eat most of them myself. I still like to cook, serve, and eat three or four vegetables at dinner, even if they don't all get eaten up, and I'm a little sad that the fresh complexity and chronic time crunch of children and a husband has reduced my average somewhat.

Like my mother before me, I believe in starting with good-tasting varieties picked at peak maturity, and I rarely use recipes. For each vegetable, I typically add one fat (butter, olive oil) and one flavor (feta, basil), and perhaps a contrasting texture (walnuts). I'm averse to any complex sequence, so I'll use one cooking method, seldom two: boil, sauté, roast, or braise. (The brown braise is an exception well worth the time. First sauté parsnip sticks in butter, then braise in cider.) Salt is indispensable with the colorful, starchy things we call vegetables. When you boil a vegetable, salt also serves to keep the proteins and other flavor agents in it, rather than allowing them to leach into the water, where they are wasted.

Perhaps above all, and not unlike the naïve fathers in *The Fantasticks*, I am a bit simple about vegetable cookery. I like to know what I am getting. I have little patience for vegetable dishes that somehow slight or smother the main character. I like to taste the beets, pumpkin, or fennel. Sexy and original combinations do not emerge from my kitchen, and my repertoire has not grown noticeably more sophisticated in twenty years of cooking. Where vegetables are concerned, I'm not a subtle person. But everyone who eats at our table asks me how to make my braised red cabbage, roasted carrots, and "those amazing onions." Now you know. Below, please find my everyday approach to the vegetables I most love.

Okra Gumbo

Mine is in no way a traditional version of this Southern classic, but I like it this way. Start with equal parts okra, sweet corn, and tomatoes. Slice the okra, take the corn off the cob, and cut the tomatoes in chunks. Sauté the corn in olive oil in a large pot. Let it brown a little; the sugar will sweeten the gumbo. Add the tomatoes and okra. Simmer about 20 minutes, until the flavors have melded and that slimy agent in okra has thickened the broth somewhat. Season. This is also tasty with strips of chicken or shrimp.

Fried Okra

Slice the okra in ½-inch rounds. Dip them in cornmeal. Heat olive oil and fry them in one layer. Do not turn until one side has colored. Season and serve at once.

Potluck Potato Salad

You can count on the high, lonesome sounds at Carl Klingler's birthday party. Carl plays the mandolin in his band, Jericho Grass, which has gigs all over the towns near Small Farm, our place in the Delaware Valley. I expected someone might pick up a fiddle and give us "Paradise" by John Prine, but I had no idea there'd be so much good food. My no-recipe potato salad is made with boiled eggs and half-peeled small red spuds and dressed with olive oil, sour cream, mustard, dill, and a splash of vinegar. Most potato salads are slick with corn-oil mayonnaise. I like lots of eggs and a sharp dressing.

Tomato Salads

In the summers of my youth, we ate tomatoes three ways and only three ways: on tomato sandwiches, which ran pink with mayonnaise; in my mother's cucumber salad with slivers of onions and a cider vinegar dressing; and sliced in large quantities with salt. I can eat tomatoes in any shape, but Rob loves thick wedges, so that is what I do, with one exception. When I serve tomatoes with buffalo mozzarella, shredded basil leaves, and good olive oil, I slice them in large rounds. For Rob's wedge salad, cut large chunks of good tomatoes and cubes of Bulgarian sheep milk feta. Dress the tomatoes and cheese right in the bowl, with olive oil, balsamic vinegar, and a tiny sprinkle of minced Greek oregano or thyme, tossing gently so that the olive oil turns slightly whitish from the crumbling cheese. In lieu of salt, consider a touch of the feta brine or black olives.

Griddled Scallions

When you go to the market in April and May, buy several bunches of bulb onions or scallions on every visit. By June, there will be so much produce you will have forgotten how desperate you were for something fresh and green. So small and delectable, griddled scallions are devoured the moment you set them out. Use the white part only, including just a bit where it turns green. If the scallions are very thick, slice them in half lengthwise. Heat the olive oil in a skillet until a drop of water sizzles noisily. Lay the onions flat, in a row, in the skillet. Salt generously. Do not turn! The first side takes a full 5 minutes to color. When the scallions are soft and brown, flip each one individually and brown the other side. Serve at once. If you are patient enough to make a very large batch, more than everyone can eat, day-old griddled scallions are delicious chopped and added to any soup, salad, or grain.

Zucchini and Yellow Squash

Cube the squash. Cut fresh (uncured) garlic in large pieces and shred basil. Heat a little too much olive oil in a skillet. The vegetables should sit in it. Scatter the squash cubes in the oil with a few grinds of unrefined sea salt. Turn the cubes when they start to color on the corners. Don't mash them up; be gentle. When the pieces are half-cooked, toss in the garlic and basil. Take the pan off the heat and move the squash to a serving dish with a slotted spoon. Don't discard the lovely oil in the pan; keep it for dressing rice or other vegetables. Serve the squash at once or tomorrow, plain or with a grating of Parmigiano-Reggiano, alone or over pasta.

Cannellini Beans with Garlic and Lemon

I like garlic, but it takes time to mince it properly, and I don't like the smell of garlic on my fingers at bedtime. To flavor these beans, I slice fresh (uncured) garlic in large pieces and let it sit in olive oil. When the oil has rested for an hour or two, I dress the beans with the oil, a squeeze of lemon juice, a sprinkle of minced parsley, and salt. I eat around the garlic; the garlicky oil is just enough for me. Count me a fan of canned chickpeas and cannellini; soaking and cooking these dried beans is not worth the trouble. Little gray-green Puy lentils, on the other hand, are easy to cook and tasty with olive oil, dried cherries, and feta cheese.

Braised Red Cabbage and Apples

Shred a red cabbage. Slice 2 onions and 2 or 3 apples. Heat plenty of olive oil in a large, heavy pan and sauté the onions and cabbage until they are half-soft. Add the apple slices. Keep stirring until all the pieces are completely soft; it will take a solid 30 minutes. Add 4 or 5 cups of cider, a cinnamon stick, perhaps a splash of red wine if you have it. Simmer until everything is very soft and the flavors have melded. Add 1 tablespoon of butter. The sauce should be thick and shiny. Season. Serve with sour cream and fat sausages. Why sauté the vegetables for so long? If they are soft, you've already sweetened the dish by removing the water; if they are undercooked when you pour in the cider, you will make boiled cabbage, something else entirely.

Sweet Potatoes with Ginger and Cream

Set the oven to 350°F. Sauté 2 onions. Peel and slice 4 or 5 sweet potatoes. Lay the potatoes in a casserole dish with butter, onions, cinnamon, chopped candied ginger, a grating of fresh nutmeg, and a grind of salt. Cover with ¼ cup of cream and bake until soft, about 30 minutes.

Roasted Carrots

Set the oven to 350°F. I prefer to roast larger, irregular, fingerlike pieces rather than coins or cubes, and this is how I cut them. Hold the carrot stick, slice off a diagonal piece, give the carrot a half turn, and slice again, as if sharpening a pencil. Put the carrots in one to two layers in an iron skillet—I usually use two pans to keep the carrots in one layer—and toss lightly with olive oil and salt. Dot the carrots with pieces of butter. Put the carrots in the oven. When they are warm, open the oven and shake or stir to cover the vegetables evenly with oil and butter. When the carrots are half-soft, add chopped parsley or thyme and stir again. When the carrots are plenty soft and a little brown on the edges, cut a juice orange in half and squeeze the juice over the pan. Put them back in the oven for a few minutes, or until the juice is gone. Season again and serve. One pound of carrots serves about four. It will take about an hour. Even supermarket carrots in the dead of winter are good this way.

Plain Roasted Beets

I start Roasted Beets with Blue Cheese and Walnuts (page 151) by roasting *chunks* of beets; I love how the sweet, wrinkly exterior catches the olive oil in that dish. But Michele Pulaski, who shares my love for beets, taught me another way to roast these red roots. Her method is simpler, and because the beets are whole, they keep well in the fridge for a host of uses. Slice off the tops and dress the beets with a little olive oil. Put them in one layer in a covered pan with a bit of water. Bake at 350°F for about an hour, or until a knife slides in easily. When the beets are cool enough to handle, hold them in a towel—a towel you don't mind getting stained carmine—and rub the skin off. The result is a silky beet with intense flavor, quite unlike a watery boiled beet. Chunks or slices of baked beets are delicious dressed with fresh orange juice, olive oil, and goat cheese.

Braised Green Wave Mustard

In the crowded field of greens with great flavor, Green Wave mustard, a favorite of my parents, is still one of the best. I love it raw on a sandwich in place of the lettuce *and* the mustard. It's fresh in April and fresh in November. Brown lots of onions sliced thin in olive oil. Chop the mustard stems small and the leaves bigger. Put the stems in the pan a few minutes before the leaves. Sauté until wilted. Add a couple of ladles of chicken stock and braise until tender. Season with salt and pepper. The leaves should be a fresh green, not overcooked in the Southern style of collards. I often add a touch of olive oil at the end. These are delicious tipped into chicken soup. A sweeter alternative: add apple slices to the onions and braise in cider.

Tiny Spicy Eggplant

Most baby—or very young—vegetables have little flavor, and I avoid them. But purple, striated Fairy Tale eggplants are not immature—they are miniature—and they're delicious. Set the oven to 300°F. Split the eggplants in half from the fat, round end to the stem, but don't cut through the stem; the halves stay connected. Split large ones in quarters. Grind unrefined sea salt, peppercorns, chili, cumin seeds, coriander seeds—just a bit of each—in a mortar and pestle; or use powdered spices. Mix the spices in olive oil and rub the paste all over the split eggplants. Roast in an iron skillet until completely soft, about 20 minutes. Don't burn the skin. Serve warm or at room temperature. Put out a dipping sauce like Tzatziki (page 119) or hummus, or make one on the spot with crème fraîche, olive oil, lemon juice, garlic, and minced oregano, thyme, or mint.

Rapini or Broccoli Rabe

A wonderful fall and winter crop, rapini also winters over, and if you're lucky, you'll find it at market for a couple of weeks in April. It's sweeter then because brassicas (including cabbage and collard greens) produce sugar as a natural, internal antifreeze. The same is true of root crops, such as turnips. I first learned this from some of our customers at the RFK Stadium market in Washington, D.C. They'd look suspiciously at our mustard, collards, and kale, and ask, "Have these greens been frozen?" First I mumbled, thinking we'd been caught doing something wrong, and then I learned to say yes, for that was not only what the ladies wanted to hear but also true.

My standard approach with all the dark, leafy greens, including beet leaves, is simple. First sauté onions or the whites of scallions in olive oil until soft. Let them color—don't flip them too soon—but don't let them burn. Remove the onions and add more oil to the oniony ambrosia. Chop the green stems in small pieces and the leaves in larger ones. Add the stems first. When they are half-tender, add the leaves. Stir it all and add the onions again. You'll need enough olive oil to coat every piece but not so much that you can't add more olive oil after you take the greens off the heat. Finish with salt, a sprinkle of cayenne pepper, and a squeeze of lemon.

Simple Carrots and Parsnips

This brilliant method marries the sweetness of carrots with any sharper root vegetable and offers a variation on the overfamiliar texture of roasted roots (chunky) and puréed ones (velvety). I learned it from Amanda Hesser, and this is how I remember (and make) it; Amanda's own instructions are lost to me. Peel equal parts parsnips and carrots and grate on the largest grater hole. Sauté in butter and perhaps a shower of diced parsley until soft. Season.

griddled red peppers

In the early years, we picked a few green bell peppers and left a few rows to ripen fully to red. We sold the green ones for twenty cents and the red ripe ones for a quarter. (I used to think of the red ones as expensive, but now I pay a buck for a red pepper.) Still, my mother's pricing—she did all the pricing—taught me that a red bell pepper is worth more than a green one. There's more vitamin C in a red pepper, but the best thing is its sweetness. A green bell pepper is sharp, grassy. Eventually we stopped picking and selling green peppers altogether and let them all ripen like tomatoes. Today I use green peppers for only two things: a little dice in Beef Chili (page 109) and griddled green peppers with onions to serve with Italian sausage. But all summer long, you will find me buying a couple of dozen red bell peppers to roast or griddle. You will never make too many; they are the first vegetable to be eaten, and if they're in the fridge, there is always hope for a superlative sandwich. When I've had my fill of griddled red peppers, I make red pepper soup. Just put them in the food processor with a clove of sautéed garlic, chicken stock, and milk or cream.

Patience is the secret to good griddled peppers. Take your time. You can get the same results by roasting them for about an hour in a 350°F oven, but I mostly use the stove; it keeps the kitchen cooler and I don't have to open the oven to shake and flip the peppers. When I use the oven, I sometimes add whole peeled garlic cloves, which soften nicely.

2 red bell peppers per person
¼ c olive oil—more or less
unrefined sea salt—perhaps a chunky grind

1. Cut off the stem and cap of the peppers at the shoulders, as if making a top for a teapot. Pop the green stem out. Pop the white seeds out of the cavity. Now wash the caps and cups, and cut flesh in long strips. In this way you preserve every millimeter of pepper flesh.
2. Heat the olive oil in a large cast-iron skillet or enamel pot.
3. Cook the peppers in one layer over low heat, turning infrequently, until they are soft and a little brown on the edges. Add oil to keep them quite moist.
4. Salt generously.
5. When you lift the peppers out of the pan into the serving bowl, there will be extra oil. You don't want to serve the peppers swimming in orange oil, but it's delicious, so keep it for another use. If you're eating the peppers today, serve them at room temperature. Otherwise, refrigerate. ✛

griddled onions

The O'Kelly family came to lunch on a cold Saturday in December. We were ten people, with five children under six, including two sets of twins. At such a party, the children are royally entertained (by each other) and I am not ambitious. All I want to accomplish is a delicious lunch that allows me to talk to Mary about being a doctor, wife, and mother. To pull that off, I chose only one dish requiring me to read a recipe. That was Pumpkin Pie Custard (page 202), which I made ahead the day before. The rest is just freelancing at the stove. We had braised chicken, mashed potatoes, and broccoli—and it was all nice. But the most popular dish was griddled onions. Mary kept asking for more, flattering it with the name "onion marmalade." Rose often asks me to make "sweet onions," and I do, year-round. Caramelized onions are a prime example of the famous Maillard reaction (page 108). Apply heat to amino acids and reducing sugars, and the result is a blast of deep flavors. Several things will accelerate the Maillard effect: limited liquid (I soften the onions well before adding a little liquid); something sweet (cider); and a pinch of baking soda (or other alkaline agent), which works but I don't use. Patience is all you do need. Even the cider is not strictly necessary; there are lots of sugars in the onions, but the cider creates a light syrup with a little shine. Another fine braising liquid is a semi-dry or dry hard cider. You can flavor these onions many ways; a winning combination is red wine, cinnamon, nutmeg, and a whisper of cumin. One more tip: make lots of onions. You just might have enough leftovers to embellish grilled cheese sandwiches, green salads, roasted vegetables, brown rice, chicken tacos, and tomato soup. My large batches with ten or twelve onions never last more than two days.

2-3 large onions per person (white, yellow, red, or Vidalia)
¼ c olive oil—more or less
1 c or so sweet or hard cider, fresh orange juice, or white wine
1 T unsalted butter
unrefined sea salt

1. Slice the onions long and thin, in pieces of equal thickness, until you are very bored and have a huge pile. (It still won't be enough.)
2. Heat the olive oil in a large pan. When it's hot, but not smoking, put the onions in one or two layers at most.
3. Cook the onions over medium heat until they are very soft, and a little brown on the edges. Check them often, but let each layer of onions color before you turn them with a wooden spoon. The onions will be pretty soft in about 30 minutes. Do not rush.
4. Add half the cider, juice, or wine. Stir as the liquid cooks off, scraping up the nice brown bits. Add the rest of the liquid and repeat.
5. Add the butter and stir. The reduced liquid and butter will make a silky sauce. The dish is ready when the onions are completely soft with brown edges. There will be no taste of juice or alcohol.
6. Salt generously.
7. Lift the onions out of the pan into a serving bowl. There will probably be a little extra oil and butter at the bottom of the pan. You don't want to serve the onions swimming in it, but it's very tasty, so keep it for another use.
8. If you are eating the onions today, serve them at room temperature. Otherwise, refrigerate. ✛

green bean salad with options

Serves 4 generously and 6 modestly

It's summer, we have guests, they include children, and we should eat close to six or everyone will be cranky by bedtime. But the days are long and lovely, and I don't want to spend two hours in the kitchen while everyone else is swimming and playing, so I'll be brutally productive. I have a plan for the center of the plate—maybe hamburgers, roast chicken, or baked salmon—but everything else will be ad hoc. Happily, the fridge is full of produce. I might put out tomatoes with a creamy burrata and ask someone to shuck corn. If there are beans in the fridge, I'll blanch them first, then toss them with sautéed garlic and Parmigiano-Reggiano, or cherry tomatoes and feta, or walnuts and blue cheese, or many other flavors. I've made these room-temperature salads countless times, and though the themes repeat, they don't wear thin.

1 lb green beans
3 T olive oil
unrefined sea salt

1. Boil lots of salted water.
2. Snap the stems off the beans and rinse them once.
3. Boil the beans in deep water until they are crisp-tender, but more tender than crisp, about 5 minutes. I like them bright green but not crunchy.
4. Drain and dress them immediately with olive oil and salt.
5. Now you can set them aside until it's time to make dinner. If you blanch them the day before, refrigerate. ✢

Usually I'll choose one cheese, one vegetable, and one herb, and see that they pair off nicely. The dressing should match, too. Consider your vinegars (red, white, Champagne, cider) and don't neglect juices (lemon, orange, cider). Just remember a ratio of four parts olive oil to one part vinegar—or even a little less vinegar. Often I dress the beans with oil first, and then dribble a few drops of vinegar, tasting as I go. In other words, you don't have to whisk dressing separately, unless it's vinaigrette, for which you first emulsify the mustard, as in Cobb Salad (page 29).

Some Winners
Parmigiano + Pine nuts + Basil (Olive oil)
Fulvi Pecorino Romano + Cherry tomatoes + New-season garlic sautéed in olive oil
Feta + Cherry tomatoes + Black olives (Olive oil + Red wine vinegar)
Young Manchego + Griddled red peppers + Marcona almonds (Olive oil + Sherry vinegar)
Pecorino + Walnuts + Basil (Olive oil)

Add Another Vegetable
Sautéed garlic
Shallots, diced small and sautéed briefly
Griddled Onions (page 139)
Griddled Red Peppers (page 137)
Raw red peppers, in fine slivers
Endive or another sturdy leaf
Cherry tomatoes cut in half
Olives

Add Some Cheese
Blue cheese, crumbled
Feta, crumbled
Parmigiano-Reggiano, shaved in large curls
Pecorino Romano, shaved in large curls
Manchego, young or aged, cut in thick matchsticks

Mince Fresh Herbs
Parsley
Dill
Summer savory

Top with Nuts
Walnuts
Pine nuts
Marcona almonds

asparagus with eggs

Serves 2 for a light lunch and 4 as a salad or first course

There are dishes I can eat again and again, like a grateful starving person, for a few short weeks, and yet during all the other long months, I live quite happily without them. This is one of those dishes. The mild spears are velvety, the yellow-cream-orange eggs rich and silky. Leaves add a crunch. As I write, the vivid greens match the lush summer jungle visible from every window. Rob and I are alone at Small Farm for two days while the children are in school in New York City—a first—and we have just met for this very lunch. Our leaves are Troutback Romaine, a red-speckled lettuce with exceptional flavor first grown in Holland in the 1600s. What is important about the dressing is the ratio of four parts oil to one part vinegar. You will have more than you need. Make less if you like, but the leftover dressing is handy. The work is in the whisking, and the dressing tastes good on everything from chicken sandwiches to egg salad. In my perfect salad, the egg yolks are dark yellow and moist in the center, somewhere between soft- and hard-cooked. The only variation on this dish I make as often, and love equally, features poached eggs; their golden liquid dresses the asparagus. On that dish, shave large scrolls of Parmigiano over everything.

4 eggs
1 lb asparagus
1 tsp Dijon mustard
2 T white wine or Champagne vinegar
8 T olive oil
salt and pepper
1 head romaine or Bibb

1. Put the eggs in a pan of cool-to-warm water. When it boils, turn off the heat and let them rest, covered, for 8 minutes. Take the eggs out, rinse them under cool water, and peel—don't delay. Even 2 more minutes resting (before rinsing) and the yolks will be fully cooked. Cut the eggs in half, leaving the yolks in place.
2. Meanwhile, boil salted water in another pan. Trim the ends off the asparagus. You can whack off all the ends in one blow while the stalks are still bunched, or bend each end sharply. Where it snaps is a good indication of the place where the tender parts end and the tougher ones begin.
3. Drop the spears gently into the boiling water and cook for 4 minutes. Lift the asparagus out immediately, drain, dress with a little olive oil, and set aside.
4. Whisk the mustard and vinegar until smooth, and then dribble in the oil little by little, whisking steadily. Season.
5. Tear the lettuce by hand, toss well with most of the dressing, and lay the leaves on a serving platter. Arrange the spears and open-faced eggs atop the salad, and drizzle a little more dressing on the eggs and asparagus. ✤

asparagus with hollandaise sauce

Serves 4

Martha Wilkie has brought many good things to my life. Her dreamy hollandaise sauce is one, her cookies (page 215) another. And more than that. She knows about things a country bumpkin like me has had to scramble to catch up on: houses and paints, eclectic furniture and architecture. She's a classy home cook and party-giver in that wonderful, old WASP way. With her quiet wisdom and equanimity, Martha is something of the sister I've been missing since losing mine at age six. I will always remember the day Martha walked up to me at a rummage sale in the basement of St. Anthony's Church on Sullivan Street. I was holding a pair of three-dollar shorts for Rose. We got to talking about my book *Real Food*, and before long she was helping me put together this beautiful book. The eggs in hollandaise sauce are barely cooked. If you're squeamish about that, Martha suggests that you first whisk the yolks in a double boiler over very low heat, stirring continuously. Then continue with the butter and lemon juice, as below. The suggestion of cayenne pepper comes from Julia Child herself.

1 lemon
3 eggs at room temperature
½ c (1 stick or 4 oz or 8 T) salted butter
salt and pepper
cayenne (optional)
1 lb asparagus

1. Juice the lemon to yield at least 1 tablespoon.
2. Separate the eggs and set aside the whites for another use.
3. In a small saucepan, melt the butter over low heat.
4. Beat the egg yolks in small bowl with a wire whisk.
5. Drizzle a small amount of the warm butter into the yolks, stirring vigorously, then alternate drizzling drops of the lemon juice with the hot butter. (Keep the butter warm as you do.)
6. Season. Add a bit more lemon juice if you like.
7. Drop the spears gently into boiling water and cook for 4 minutes. Lift the asparagus out immediately, drain, and dress with warm hollandaise sauce. If the sauce gets too thick from resting as you prepare the rest of the meal, add a few drops of warm water and stir. ✛

smashed & braised new potatoes

Serves 4

When I lived in London, I loved to listen to *Veg Talk* on Radio 4. Greengrocer Charlie Hicks and Greg Wallace, an East Ender and former costermonger (street vendor), gave a performance something like what you hear from the brothers Magliozzi on NPR's *Car Talk*. Both acts are homey, brash, encouraging for the home cook or home mechanic. I can still picture myself listening to the radio in the white kitchen of my house on St. Paul Street in Islington, a few blocks from the first farmers' market I opened in London. And I remember the very day I scribbled down this recipe from a *Veg Talk* caller. It was June, new potato season. Do wait for small new potatoes in your region; they are sweeter than potatoes from Far Away. Fingerlings are also good for this dish.

1 lb new potatoes
¼ c olive oil
2 T butter
unrefined sea salt
½–1 c dry white wine
parsley, tarragon, or rosemary (optional)

1. Bash the potatoes with a rolling pin on a wooden cutting board or counter so they're cracked, but not entirely in pieces. The occasional little piece is fine.
2. Heat the olive oil, butter, and salt in a lidded skillet large enough to take the potatoes in one layer. Sauté the potatoes until they start to color. Strain away any excess fat.
3. Turn up the heat, add the wine, and cover promptly. Don't allow steam to escape.
4. Cook the potatoes until they are fork-tender, turning them as needed to brown them on all sides, with lots of caramel patches. Add a splash of wine if the pan is too dry. Scrape up the brown bits on the pan as you cook and when you put them in the serving dish.
5. Serve at once with the (optional) minced herbs. ✣

broccoli with cheese sauce

Serves 4

For some reason, I always remember this classic, roux-based sauce with cheese for broccoli and cauliflower, but it's good on lots of things, like grilled zucchini or noodles. The better the cheese, the better it'll taste. Use a fairly sharp cheddar, like Prairie Breeze or Tickler, and a smooth alpine cheese, such as Swiss Gruyère, French Comté, or American Rupert from Consider Bardwell Farm. This is a wonderful side dish at Thanksgiving, and I often make more sauce to feed more people. To dress four heads of broccoli or three heads of cauliflower—and serve twelve—the proportions are three-quarters of a pound of cheese, three tablespoons of butter and flour, and one and one half cups of milk. There—now you don't have to do the math.

2 large heads broccoli (or 1 head cauliflower)
¼ lb cheddar
¼ lb Gruyère or similar
2 T butter
2 T white flour
1 c milk
black pepper
1 nutmeg
pinch of cayenne

1. Cut the broccoli (or cauliflower) in florets of even size and boil a large pot of salted water.
2. Grate the cheeses to yield a generous cup of each.
3. Gently melt the butter in a pan. Add the flour and make a roux, stirring constantly for about 10 minutes over low heat. Don't let it color.
4. When the taste of raw flour is mostly gone, gradually add the milk, whisking as you do. Cook for a few minutes, until the sauce is thick and just starting to bubble, stirring constantly.
5. Add the cheeses, turn off the heat, and stir gently until the cheeses disappear. Don't whisk. The desired effect is velvety.
6. Season with black pepper, nutmeg (I suggest grating just under half the nut), and cayenne to taste (I like ¼ teaspoon, but most children probably won't).
7. Drop the florets in the boiling salted water, cook until fork-tender, and drain.
8. Put the vegetables in a serving dish. Spoon the sauce on them and stir very gently. ✢

cauliflower fried in parmigiano

Serves 4

An orange cauliflower, crunchy with browned cheese, would look beautiful here. You can toast the pine nuts in a dry skillet, but most people (including me) brown them too much for my taste; they taste burnt, and I sometimes prefer the clean, piney flavor of the raw thing. Moreover, the dish itself overrunneth with nuttiness, from the cauliflower to the cheeses. Butter (rather than olive oil) makes it nuttier yet. This is nice next to wild salmon. You'll probably have a little more cheese than you need for one head of cauliflower, but there's no point in ordering less than a half pound of cheese at the counter.

1 head cauliflower
½ lb Parmigiano-Reggiano
½ lb Asiago
1 small bunch parsley
¼ c olive oil
1 egg
handful of capers
½ c pine nuts
black pepper

1. Cut the cauliflower in small florets: Put the brainy-looking top on the counter, with the stem to the ceiling. Cut each little branch at its base, working in a circular fashion from the bottom to top. If you cut each branch carefully, you won't hack into the florets, leaving little bits of cauliflower dust all over.
2. Grate the cheeses and mix them.
3. Chop the parsley.
4. Heat the olive oil in a large skillet.
5. Whisk the egg with a little water, no more than ¼ cup.
6. With your hands, toss the cauliflower in the egg.
7. Toss the florets with the grated cheese and parsley.
8. Fry the cauliflower until the pieces are soft to the fork and golden brown. Don't flip too often; let each piece color first.
9. Move the cauliflower to a serving dish. Scatter it with capers and pine nuts, grind plenty of black pepper, and serve at once. ✛

ratatouille

Serves 6 to 8

A late-summer staple, ratatouille requires a lot of chopping but no special skill or care. It makes excellent leftovers and delicious pasta sauce. Apart from basil, the particular herbs don't matter much. But homemade or good store-bought passata makes all the difference; otherwise, it's just roasted Italian vegetables, not the melded magic you're seeking. You will need a large glass or ceramic baking dish, perhaps two. If the mixture is too deep, it will be soupy.

1 large handful basil leaves

1 sprig thyme

1 sprig oregano

8 cloves garlic

6 T olive oil

2-3 eggplants

3 zucchini

2 red or yellow bell peppers

6 tomatoes

1 onion

½ c passata (recipe follows)

¾ tsp unrefined sea salt

1. Set the oven to 350°F.
2. Save a little fresh basil to garnish. Chop the basil roughly and mince the thyme and oregano. Slice the garlic cloves. Cover the herbs and garlic with the olive oil in a large ceramic baking dish.
3. While the olive oil is infusing, cut up the vegetables. Cut the eggplant, zucchini, and peppers in long strips. Cut the tomatoes in chunks and slice the onion.
4. Add the vegetables, the passata, and the salt to the garlic and herbs and slosh it all around. Bake it for 90 minutes to 2 hours, or until the vegetables are meltingly tender.
5. Serve hot or cold. Serve it the next day if you can, with fresh basil to garnish. ✦

passata

This plain Italian tomato sauce comes bottled, often with basil. It's handy and affordable. It's also easy to make and a great way to use surplus tomatoes in late summer. A good, quick, and affordable substitute for passata is a can of tomatoes. Run the tomatoes through a food processor or a hand mill with a little of their juice.

3 lbs tomatoes
20 basil leaves

Peel the tomatoes. Boil water in a large pot. Fill a large bowl with cold water.
Cut an X in the skin on the blossom end, opposite the stem. Drop the tomatoes in batches into the boiling water for 30 seconds. Remove the tomatoes with a slotted spoon and put them in the cold water. When they're cool enough to handle, peel the skin, cut out the stem, and scoop out the seeds. Boil the tomatoes with a little salt until they're soft. Add the basil when the tomatoes are nearly ready. Purée. Passata stays fresh in the fridge for a week and freezes well.

roasted beets with blue cheese & walnuts

Serves 4

Chefs do lots of little things with this classic—I've had it with chèvre, pistachios, and fresh orange juice—but I like it the traditional way. The beets must be cut evenly and properly roasted; they will shrink, get wrinkles, and become sweeter, and that will make all the difference. They are not to be boiled. The beets are delicious made a day ahead. Roast the beets and dress them, but don't add the blue cheese and walnuts until you serve it. This salad looks and tastes lovely served on a bed of bitter greens such as endive or radicchio (photo on page 126).

2 lbs beets
olive oil
red wine vinegar
balsamic vinegar
salt and pepper
¼ lb blue cheese
1 c raw or brined and roasted walnuts (page 21)
parsley or chives (optional)

1. Set the oven to 350°F.
2. If the skins are very tough—but only then—peel the beets. Cut the beets in chunks of even thickness.
3. Put the beets in one or at most two layers in a cast-iron skillet or skillets, coat lightly but thoroughly with olive oil, and roast until they are soft, at least 45 minutes. (A young June beet will be less dense than an old October one.) They should be fork-tender.
4. Make a dressing with four parts olive oil to one part vinegar, using half red wine vinegar and half balsamic, and season. Toss the beets with the dressing. Season again.
5. Break up the blue cheese. Gently mix the blue cheese and walnuts into the beets. If you overdo it, the cheese gets all smushed and pink. Top with chopped herbs if you like. ✛

vegetables & turkey

Thanksgiving is bombastic. There is too much food. There is no thoughtful succession of courses to ease you through the feast—just one bulging buffet. There are too many unique must-have items on the table. Cousin Lucy loves parsnips, and Uncle Bill always wants green beans. There is repetition in flavor, texture, and plant part. (Sweet potatoes, white potatoes, parsnips—three roots. Then, soft stuffing.) There are too many desserts, and they are too like the side dishes. (Velvety, spicy.) There are too many people at the table—and at the folding tables, and on the couches. And everyone is so sentimental about this or that bit.

I sound like one of those people who doesn't like the beach. (They're always whining about the salt, sand, and sun.) I love my family and I love Thanksgiving. But the way it's often done doesn't match the way I like to shop, cook, host, or eat.

It's not difficult to identify each problem and its cause. The turkey, a perfectly nice meat, is dry because it's too big. The vegetables are cold or overdone because no cook can produce six perfectly-turned-out vegetable dishes at once with one fridge and four burners. The desserts—each a tasty autumn classic—don't complement the meal. Instead, they overload it.

As a single girl, my dash past the bombast was to give a smallish dinner party. I'd edit the meal sharply and finish with one lovely dessert, like a pecan tart. Those minimalist, though not effortless, dinners in Brussels, London, and New York were a pleasure, but once I grew up, I could not avoid hosting "real" family Thanksgivings, with children of all ages, and they are somewhat messier. The most tactile memory of hosting my first Thanksgiving at Small Farm is the heavy breathing. I was only days pregnant with Rose and Jacob and already panting like a dog on an August sidewalk in Texas.

It's a seasonal festival, and the season is your ally. Start by ditching the green beans if they're not fresh in your region. Or serve September beans you cleverly pickled with dill. Make bitter rapini with garlic or red cabbage braised with apples. If a green salad can't be had at your local market or doesn't match your aesthetic, make a crunchy celeriac remoulade.

Let the vegetables represent all parts of the plant: root, stem, leaf. Let each one bring a new color and texture to the table. Plan to make two sides ahead (like the mash or creamed pearl onions) and two closer to the last minute. (Stop at four.) Dress each vegetable with one fat and one unique flavor. Puréed sweet potatoes get ginger and butter; roasted parsnips, rosemary and olive oil; creamed spinach, a dusting of nutmeg.

Let it be fun before dinner. Serve a hard cider with a little sparkle from Eve's Cidery or invent a dry seasonal cocktail and make a pitcher—maybe a rosemary-infused gin and tonic, a vodka gimlet with cranberries, or a sparkler of pear brandy and ginger ale.

Oh yes, the turkey. Order a heritage turkey raised on pasture for better texture and flavor. Buy extra necks and feet, and make the gravy in advance; otherwise, you have to stand there in your party dress, stirring the pan drippings while the turkey dries out and the guests drink your cocktail. Make a loose plan for the stuffing base (cornbread or bread crumbs) and flavor (rosemary, sage, apple), but don't fret over details; stuffing is forgiving. Remember that a turkey is not some exotic meat you've never cooked before—it is not an ostrich or alligator. It's a large chicken. Buy a small bird so you can cook it perfectly, timed to be just roasted when you sit down, not an hour before. If your crowd is large, make two eight-pound turkeys, the better to deliver crispy skin and moist meat. When the smallest and best turkey I can buy is a free-ranging butterball, a plump-breasted, white twenty-pounder, I treat it very simply. No stuffing. Rub it with olive oil and salt, set it on a rack, and roast it at 350°F for two and half hours, until the juices run clear. Let it rest.

One year—perhaps this year—be bold. Make an offbeat dessert: maple-pecan sugar cookies or a Lemon Curd Tart (page 205). If you do it with style, no one will have the nerve to complain.

mashed potatoes

Serves 6

Gone are the days when giant russets alone roamed the greengrocers. Now there are all kinds of good potatoes for mashing, frying, and baking, and some are all-rounders. My favorite is still the Yukon Gold, bred in southern Ontario for homesick Dutch and Belgian potato farmers, with a family tree including a classic Peruvian spud. It's large and smooth, and the tasty flesh really is gold. You'll need about one large potato per person. Mashed potatoes will take as much milk (or cream) as you give them, and they will need more just to soften and warm up if you make this dish the day before. If you are serving this dish right away, add warm milk as you mash, so that you don't cool them down. Whether serving our family or a crowd, I always make a large batch. I can only manage a small scoop, but other appetites are heartier and certain dishes, including three you'll find in this book, demand them: meatloaf (page 106), brisket (page 105), beef Burgundy (page 102).

3 lbs Yukon Gold potatoes
olive oil (optional)
1 tsp unrefined sea salt
¼ c (½ stick or 2 oz or 4 T) butter
2-4 c milk
cream (optional)
black pepper

1. Peel the potatoes and cut them into large chunks.
2. Boil a large pot of salted water and cook the potatoes until they are fork-tender.
3. You can pause here; in that case, coat the potatoes with a little olive oil and set aside.
4. When you are ready to mash the potatoes, add the salt.
5. Cut the butter in chunks and mash it into the potatoes with a hand masher. Add some of the milk as you go.
6. Keep mashing and keep adding milk (or cream).
7. When the potatoes are smooth, but not too smooth, season. ✦

roasted sweet potatoes

Serves any number

These orange cubes are like marshmallows with a crispy skin. Butter is always an option—and I love it slathered on a soft whole baked sweet spud—but for these, I like olive oil best. Do they get crispier with oil? Perhaps; I'm not sure. If you're making something tropical, try coconut oil. Roasted sweet potatoes are the secret in Quinoa with Roasted Vegetables (page 164). You will make these again and again—and never see leftovers.

1 sweet potato per person
¼ c olive oil
unrefined sea salt

1. Set the oven to 325°F.
2. Peel the potatoes if the peel looks old and tough. Cut the potatoes in 1-inch (or slightly smaller) cubes or thick matchsticks. What matters is that the pieces are the same size.
3. Toss the potatoes in olive oil, coating the chunks thoroughly.
4. Toss again with salt.
5. Roast for 30 to 45 minutes, until they are soft through and evenly crispy on all sides. ✢

rebbie's root gratin

Serves 4

In April 2003, I moved into the first house I'd ever owned, a small town house on Monroe Street, in Washington, D.C. In June, I opened my first American farmers' market, three convenient blocks away. Happy at last—settled. Then the fabled New York City Greenmarket made me an offer I could not resist—to reform its fifty-some farmers' markets—and on July 3, I moved to Gotham City. My time at Greenmarket was also somewhat fabled, but that's another story. Back in Washington, happily, the Mount Pleasant Farmers' Market thrived without me. First a former cookbook editor named Robin Shuster ran it beautifully. Eventually I sold it to a tall, blonde dynamo named Rebbie Higgins, who had met my mother on a train. (It's characteristic of my mother to pick up great people.) Rebbie wrote this basic gratin method for her typically effervescent fall market newsletter. To inspire the spontaneity that is the essence of market cooking, Rebbie suggests these combinations: butternut, apple, and walnut; sweet potato and pecan; potato, bacon, goat cheese, and leek; sweet potato, coconut milk, ginger, garlic, and cilantro. Like other great melding dishes, this is even better the next day.

1 lb winter vegetables (your choice)

2-4 c milk, cream, chicken broth, or vegetable stock, or any combination

¼ tsp unrefined sea salt

2-3 leeks or onions (your choice)

2 cloves garlic (optional)

2 T olive oil or unsalted butter

small handful of parsley, rosemary, or thyme (your choice)

2 slices bread

¼ lb cheddar, Gruyère, or chèvre (your choice)

¼ lb Parmigiano-Reggiano

fresh nutmeg, paprika, or cayenne (your choice)

black pepper

1. Set the oven to 400°F.
2. Slice the winter vegetables in pieces of equal thickness.
3. Salt the liquid of choice and gently simmer the rounds for about 10 minutes.
4. Meanwhile, chop the leeks or onions and the garlic. Heat the oil or butter in a pan and sauté the leeks or onions until they are soft but not brown. When they are half-soft, add the garlic.
5. Chop the herbs.
6. Toast the bread and make bread crumbs. (I use a food processor.)
7. Roughly grate the cheddar or Gruyère or crumble the chèvre.
8. Butter a baking dish. Layer the vegetables (reserving the liquid), the herbs, and the melting cheeses (cheddar, Gruyère, or chèvre) in the dish, finishing with a layer of potato or other firm root vegetable.
9. Pour most of the liquid in which you simmered the vegetables into the cracks. You'll be the judge of how much. Too much liquid and it's soupy; too little and it's dry.
10. Sprinkle with the bread crumbs, then the Parmigiano.
11. Bake for about 30 minutes or until it's bubbly, browned, and tender. Serve today or tomorrow. ✛

root vegetable purée

Serves 8

The perfect winter vegetable dish, all the better with good milk or stock.

6 lbs winter roots, such as Yukon Gold potatoes, celeriac, and parsnips
4 c chicken stock, milk, or cream, or a combination
salt and pepper

1. Peel and chop the vegetables. You must really pare down celeriac, which is very knobbly, to get to the smooth, tasty bits, and it's worth it, because the hint of celery lifts the rest of the roots, which are sweet.
2. Boil the chopped vegetables in lots of salted water until they are soft.
3. Put them in food processor and thin with a little of the cooking liquid plus chicken stock, milk, cream, or all of the above.
4. Make it one day before and warm it up with more liquids. Season.
5. Serve alone or spoon it into shallow bowls, make a little well, and put Coq au Vin (page 97) on top. ✢

sweet onion custard

Serves 8

Once I tasted this custard, which comes from Michele Pulaski, I knew I would make it many times. It's fluffy yet creamy, savory and sweet at once. It goes with anything, in any season. I like to add a little cayenne. A salty touch is also welcome: try capers, chopped olives, or diced cooked shrimp. For parties, Michele spreads the batter on sheets of puff pastry and bakes it at 350°F. Cut the squares and pass them around with drinks.

3 Vidalia (or other sweet) onions
sprigs of fresh thyme
2 T butter
1 c Parmigiano-Reggiano
3 eggs
2 c cream or 1 c cream and 1 c milk
salt and pepper

1. Set the oven to 350°F.
2. Slice the onions in thin pieces and pull the leaves off the thyme, leaving no stems.
3. Heat the butter and brown the onions slowly and patiently; don't flip them until they color. When the onions are half-soft, add the thyme.
4. When the onions are completely soft and golden, let them cool and then chop them roughly.
5. Grate the cheese.
6. Separate two eggs and set the whites aside for another use. Whisk the whole egg and two yolks.
7. Combine the cream, or cream and milk, eggs, and the cheese and mix well.
8. Add the onions, season, and mix well.
9. Spoon into eight 4-ounce glass or ceramic ramekins.
10. Bake until the custard is firm and golden, 20 to 30 minutes. ✚

an approach to brown rice

You can make brown rice exactly as the package instructs, but I like to soak it first, for two reasons. Soaking reduces the phytic acid—an anti-nutrient in plants that decreases the absorption of minerals—and it enhances the digestibility of this complex carbohydrate. Soaking also reduces the cooking time, which wreaks variability (but not quite havoc) on the water-to-rice ratio the label commands. So I don't measure rice or water, and I cook each batch ad hoc. Perhaps it sounds like more work to check it a few times, usually adding a little more water, but it suits me because I cannot predict how moist the rice is (older rice is drier) and the soaking time varies with my day. I'm often pleased with soft and moist rice for dishes like chicken stir-fry and tomato soup. My husband prefers the grains dry and separate; for that effect, I don't soak it first, and I put a towel under the lid of the enamel pot to create a steamy interior. I like organic American brown rice, both long and short grain, and stubby arborio.

Rinse and soak a few scoops of brown rice in water for perhaps 6 hours or overnight. Drain and rinse it in a fine colander. Warm 2 or 3 tablespoons of butter or olive oil in a large pot. (Here is the moment to color diced onions fully; then add the rice.) Gently heat the rice in the oil or butter until a nutty fragrance wafts up. This will keep the grains distinct. Pour in water or chicken stock to a level about ½ inch above the rice. Add ¼ teaspoon of unrefined sea salt and simmer uncovered for 20 to 30 minutes. Stir to prevent sticking and add more water if necessary. When the rice is tender, drain any excess water. Sometimes I turn off the heat, cover the pan, and let the rice absorb a small amount of extra water. Mount with butter or olive oil.

Now dress it anyway you like or leave it be. A memorable, ad lib combination was inspired by Mediterranean pilafs. Soak dried apricots in water, keep the liquid, and chop the fruit. Toss the hot rice with butter, minced parsley, cumin, toasted pine nuts, the softened apricots and a little of their sweet liquid, and chicken stock.

quinoa

Serves 2

1 c quinoa
1 ¼ c salted water or chicken stock
½ tsp unrefined sea salt
1 T olive oil
salt and pepper

A whole-foodist from the beginning, my mother was always game for what you might call hippie or homestead cooking. So in my youth, many food experiments visited our homemade wooden shelves, fridge, and pantry. She made kombucha (once) and beer (as often). There was wheat germ, blackstrap molasses, brewer's yeast, a wheat grinder for pancakes, and all manner of less-famous brown seeds. Yet she was never sanctimonious, and I remember how we laughed at one label: QUINOA: ANCIENT SUPERGRAIN OF THE FUTURE. Now, of course, these foods are chic—as is my mother. The seeds of quinoa, a staple crop in the Andes, caught the eye of the baby food industry because they're fairly rich in protein, fats, minerals, and vitamins. The food chemists also know that quinoa contains a family of chemicals called saponins (which taste soapy and bitter) and phytic acid, an anti-nutrient that reduces absorption of protein and minerals—not so good for baby food. The answer is simple: soak and rinse it. This removes most of the saponins, for better flavor, and reduces the phytic acid, enhancing the nutrition. Quinoa—a little spiral of nuttiness in red, black, or mahogany—is delicious. Just know that eggs, milk, yogurt, butter, avocado, and fish roe are richer in protein, fats, minerals, and vitamins—and therefore better baby foods.

1. Soak the quinoa in water for 30 minutes or longer. (Overnight will not hurt it.)
2. Rinse it well in warm water for 3 or 4 minutes, using a fine colander or cheesecloth, lest you lose the tiny seeds.
3. Put the quinoa in the water or stock and bring it to a boil. Reduce the heat and simmer for 10 to 15 minutes, until the seeds are tender. Drain any excess water. How much liquid is left will depend on the quinoa and how long it soaked.
4. Remove the pan from the heat and let it sit for 5 minutes.
5. Fluff the quinoa with fork. Add the olive oil and season. ✢

quinoa with roasted vegetables

Serves 8

Follow two tips for this dish and they will all be raving. Cube the sweet potatoes with care and watch them closely. When overcooked, they are dry and hard; they should be crispy outside and silky inside.

Take your time with the Griddled Onions, and make a lot of them. You cannot add too many to this dish, but extras won't be wasted either. Nearly any vegetable would be tasty here. Just make sure it's perfectly cooked before you add it to the quinoa. You can cook all the vegetables and the quinoa a day ahead and assemble it later.

3 c red quinoa

6 onions

3 sweet potatoes

1 bunch swiss chard or 1 lb spinach or 1 bunch rapini

3 T olive oil for sautéing

½ c pine nuts

½ c olive oil

1 T cider vinegar

1 T cider

½ c dried cherries, raisins, or apricots (diced)

salt and pepper

1. Cook the quinoa (page 163).
2. Griddle the onions (page 139).
3. Bake the sweet potatoes (page 157).
4. Cook the green vegetable just right. If it's a leaf-and-stem plant such as beet greens, Swiss chard, rapini, or beet greens, be sure to chop the stems smaller and the leaves bigger. Separate the two. Heat some olive oil and sauté the stems first. Then add the leaves.
5. Gently toast the pine nuts in a dry skillet until they are just barely golden.
6. Whisk the olive oil, cider vinegar, and cider.
7. Mix all the ingredients and season. Serve warm or at room temperature. ✢

barbecue at small farm

citrus-chili charred chicken

corn spoon

apple crisp with vanilla bean ice cream

lemonade with blueberry syrup

citrus-chili charred chicken

Serves 10

Here's another winner from Michele Pulaski. Most of the work in this dish is done in advance, and time does the rest. It's meant to be charred, and that means firing up the grill. It's also delicious baked in a 400°F oven for about an hour, though you'll miss the charring. The marinade easily flavors chicken to serve ten or twelve. You won't regret leftovers. Adobo merits a word or two. The word itself means marinade; it derives from the old Spanish for "stew," *adobar*, and dates to antiquity. Before refrigeration, cooks on the Iberian peninsula used adobo to preserve meat; today, of course, a marinade adds flavor and tenderness. Recipes vary, but traditional adobo contains antibacterial paprika, which lends the powder a strong reddish-orange tint. Capsaicins in paprika cause fats to dissolve, allowing flavors to penetrate the tissue, and vinegar or citrus makes the meat tender. It's not easy to find a clean, organic adobo paste. Try Lodo Red adobo powder, which includes chili powder, Spanish paprika, shallots, Mexican oregano, green onion, cumin, and cloves. To make a paste for marinating any meat, poultry, or fish, simply mix the powder with cider vinegar, oil, and water.

2 dried ancho peppers
4-5 oranges, lemons, and limes
1 red onion
1 shallot
3 cloves garlic
1 small bunch oregano
1 branch rosemary
1 small bunch cilantro
5 canned chipotle peppers
2 tsp Lodo Red adobo powder
½ c cider vinegar
1 c olive oil
2 T red pepper flakes
1 tsp black pepper
15 chicken thighs, breasts, and drumsticks (with bones and skin)

1. Cover the anchos with water for at least 10 minutes and chop them. Keep the seeds.
2. Use a glass or stainless steel bowl or shallow dish large enough to hold the chicken. You may need two. Add each ingredient to the dish as you prepare it.
3. Zest and juice the citrus.
4. Chop the onion, shallot, and garlic.
5. Strip and roughly chop the herbs. The cilantro stems can stay.
6. Add all the remaining ingredients except the chicken to the bowl and mix.
7. Slip the chicken parts into the marinade and refrigerate overnight. Rearrange the chicken so that each piece is well soaked.
8. Grill it. ✛

corn spoon

Serves 8 to 10

"Promise me," I used to say to Rob, "that we'll never get married and never split up." And he would. But when Jacob and Rose were five days old, he popped the question in front of Julian, who looked up from his lunch. I was flabbergasted and said yes. We settled on August, largely (as I saw it) so we could get married on the lawn at Small Farm and eat my favorite seasonal produce: peaches, corn, tomatoes. Our friend Bill Niman promised to send us the first batch of grass-fattened tenderloin beef from his home ranch. A salad of good mozzarella with my parents' own Virginia tomatoes and local basil would be easy. But what's an elegant corn dish? I didn't know, but Michele Pulaski, who catered our wedding, knew just the thing. She made her fluffy, addictive corn spoon, also known as sweet corn pudding. How sweet it was. Buy four to six ears of corn; one large perfect ear yields about one cup of kernels. In the winter, you can use frozen corn; thaw it first. I make it in a 10-inch cast-iron skillet because I like the browned edges, but any baking dish will do.

4 c fresh (or frozen) corn kernels

¼ c (½ stick or 2 oz or 4 T) unsalted butter plus some for the skillet

4 eggs

1 c cream

½ c milk

6 T organic whole cane sugar

2 T flour

2 tsp Bob's Red Mill baking powder

1 tsp unrefined sea salt

1. Set the oven to 350°F.
2. Cut the corn off the cobs to yield 4 cups. Blend 2 cups in the food processor.
3. Melt the ¼ cup of butter in the skillet (or baking dish).
4. Thoroughly mix the puréed corn, melted butter, eggs, cream, milk, and sugar.
5. Mix the dry ingredients well.
6. Mix the wet and dry ingredients and the whole corn.
7. Butter the bottom and sides of the skillet.
8. Pour the batter into the skillet. Bake it until the top is brown and the center is just set, about 45 minutes. Cool for 10 minutes and serve. ✢

apple crisp

Serves 8

Michele Pulaski's sweet, crumbly topping, which I've tinkered with just slightly—suggesting a touch less sugar, a grating of nutmeg—adorns any tree fruit or berry with style. With peaches, plums, and other softer fruit, consider ripeness carefully. A mix of dead-ripe, just-ready, and one-day-early stone fruit ensures a balance. If they're all dead-ripe for eating, the fruit filling is too syrupy. As usual, the total quantity of sugar is in your hands. You'll need an 8-inch-square ceramic baking dish and a baking sheet. Serve it with Vanilla Bean Ice Cream (page 220) or Crème Anglaise (page 214).

2 lbs pretty-ripe apples

2 tsp cinnamon

1¼ cup King Arthur white whole wheat flour

½ c whole rolled oats

½ tsp unrefined sea salt

1 nutmeg

1 c (2 sticks or 8 oz or 16 T) chilled butter

½–¾ c muscovado sugar

½–¾ c organic whole cane sugar

1. Set the oven to 350°F.
2. Slice the apples in the baking dish and mix with 1 teaspoon of the cinnamon.
3. Mix the flour, the oats, the second teaspoon of cinnamon, the salt, and a grating of nutmeg in a bowl.
4. Get the butter out of the fridge. In another bowl, cut the butter into cubes with a pastry cutter or two butter knives. Mix the sugars and butter.
5. Combine the wet and dry ingredients with your hands until the bits of butter are pea-sized and well coated.
6. Gently press the topping on the apples. Pinch and poke the crumble to give it texture and crunchy clusters. Do not flatten it.
7. Set the dish on a baking sheet to catch leaks. Bake for about 35 minutes, until the topping is brown and the juices are brown and bubbly. ✢

lemonade with blueberry syrup

Makes 12 small (4 ounce) or 6 large (8 ounce) drinks

Roll the lemons on the counter firmly before cutting them so they'll juice more easily.

8 Meyer lemons
6 cups still or sparkling water
2-3 T organic whole cane sugar
blueberry syrup (page 11)
mint

1. Juice the lemons. Add sugar and mix well.
2. Add a splash of blueberry syrup to the bottom of a pitcher or each glass and top with a leaf of mint. ✢

essential breads

yogurt biscuits

Makes 6 large or 8 small biscuits.

This is a bread with quite a lot of butter in the dough, best eaten with more butter on the hot item itself. Buttermilk biscuits are traditional, but I seldom have buttermilk on hand. There's always yogurt in the fridge, and the effect is the same: the acidic liquid makes the dough rise. The sugar and crème fraîche are optional but delicious, and once I used Maple Hill Creamery yogurt lightly sweetened with maple syrup, and the biscuits were luxe–better than cake. We buy only unsalted butter, but salted butter makes a breakfast biscuit shine. For strawberry shortcake, cut one quart of berries in half and sprinkle with a tablespoon of sugar. Let them stand for at least 30 minutes. Serve the berries on hot, split biscuits with whipped cream.

½ c (1 stick or 4 oz or 8 T) cold salted butter plus extra for the pan

2 c white flour plus extra for rolling

2 T Bob's Red Mill baking powder

1 tsp salt

1 T organic whole cane sugar (optional)

1 c yogurt

1 T crème fraîche (optional)

1. Set the oven to 450°F.
2. Cut the butter in chunks and put it in the fridge or freezer. The harder, the better.
3. Butter a glass dish or cast iron skillet. Use a 9-inch round skillet or a 9-inch square dish–or something smaller, so they're crammed in and rise up tall.
4. Mix the dry ingredients thoroughly in a bowl.
5. Put the flour mix in a food processor. Add the cold butter pieces and pulse until they are the size of blueberries. (You can also cut the butter in with a pastry cutter or two butter knives.) Be light and speedy. Do not overwork the dough.
6. Turn the dough into a large bowl.
7. Is the oven at 450°F yet? Do not mix the wet and dry ingredients until the oven is ready!
8. Add the wet ingredients to the dough and mix *quickly* with a fork. (The baking powder and yogurt begin to react when they touch. Biscuits should rise in the oven, not in the bowl.)
9. Flour the counter and tip the shaggy dough out of the bowl. Form a loose layer of dough 2 to 3 inches thick. Using more flour on your hands, tidy up the sides a bit, but just a bit. Work quickly. It will look a little like a down comforter.
10. Cut out the biscuits with a quick turn of a biscuit cutter or floured glass.
11. Set each biscuit close to the next so they puff up rather than spread out.
12. Bake until they are golden and puffy, about 10 to 12 minutes. ✛

irish soda bread with muesli

Serves 6 to 8

Mother Linda is a travel and cooking maven who loves real food. Her people are Irish, so one of her obsessions is finding the Ultimate Irish Soda Bread.

No such animal, I suspect, but meanwhile she's gathered a collection of family favorites. This one she wangled from an Irish cook who happened to sit next to her on a plane. The lady recited it from memory. Says Mother Linda, "If you are lucky enough to have a source of raw milk, measure the required amount and set it in a warm place overnight to sour. You sour the milk to produce lactic acid to react with the alkaline baking soda, which produces carbon dioxide to raise the bread." The simple chemistry of yeast-free baking! You will need parchment paper and a flat baking sheet.

3 c spelt flour or sprouted spelt flour or 2 ¾ c King Arthur whole wheat flour

2 c Bob's Red Mill muesli

1 tsp Bob's Red Mill baking soda

¼ c (½ stick or 2 oz or 4 T) unsalted butter

1 egg

1 ½ c buttermilk, soured raw milk, or yogurt (and perhaps a little extra)

1. Set the oven to 375°F.
2. In a large bowl, mix the flour, muesli, and baking soda.
3. Cut the butter into small pieces. Pinch those into smaller pieces as you work the butter into the flour with your fingers. It's ready when the texture is grainy.
4. Whisk the egg and buttermilk. Pour the wet mixture into the dry ingredients and mix to make a thick, moist dough. Be ready to add a little more liquid if necessary.
5. Turn the dough out on a floured piece of parchment paper and shape it into a round loaf.
6. Put the parchment paper on a baking sheet, set the loaf on it, and cut a cross on the top of the dough.
7. Bake for 1 hour, or until a toothpick comes out clean.
8. Cover with a cloth and cool overnight. ✢

isabel scanlon's irish soda bread

Serves 6 to 8

Before our young Waldorf school found a home on Avenue B in the East Village, Eamon and Mary O'Kelly hosted various toddlers, along with their own twins, Aedan and Niahm, in their apartment.

When Rose and Jacob were tiny, the school also spent a few months at our place. Each morning the teachers would get the wood furniture, polished stones, sheepskins, and silks out of our hall bathtub and redecorate the living room. As the children arrived, mothers, fathers, and nannies would sidle along to our tiny back room. Our school did not have the appropriate license for children to be dropped off, so we had to hide on-site. Mostly we gossiped, interrupted now and then by a weepy cherub. Sometimes Mary would bring her mother's soda bread. When you have a three-year-old and newborn twins, it may sound saintly to invite the whole school, plus parents and nannies, to your place. Quite the opposite; it was good for me. Each morning Julian's friends came to him, and mine to me. Nothing better than the company of mothers when your only job is nursing two babies.

1 T unsalted butter
4 c white whole wheat flour
⅓ c organic whole cane sugar
2 tsp Bob's Red Mill baking powder
1 tsp Bob's Red Mill baking soda
pinch of salt
2 eggs
1 c sour cream
1 ¼ c good buttermilk, such as Kate's
½ to 1 c raisins (optional)

1. Set the oven to 350°F.
2. Soften the butter. Coat the bottom and sides of a 9- or 10-inch springform cake pan and dust with flour.
3. Mix or sift the flour, sugar, baking powder, baking soda, and salt.
4. In another bowl, whisk the eggs. Add the sour cream, buttermilk, and (optional) raisins. Mix.
5. When the oven is hot, mix the wet and dry ingredients with a spoon, adding a little buttermilk if the batter is dry. Says Mary, "The nature of the batter is gluey, lumpy, and sticky. It pours with the help of a wooden spoon."
6. Pour the batter into the pan and bake for about an hour, until a knife or toothpick comes out dry.
7. Let the loaf stand until it's cool. Open the pan and turn the bread out onto a clean towel.
8. Leave the bread covered with the towel for about an hour. Otherwise (say my Irish sources) it will crumble when sliced. ✢

cornbread

Serves 8 to 10

Once again, I've been defeated by popular opinion at home. I like a corny, savory, rugged corn bread, with a touch of honey and cayenne pepper. No one else eats it, not even hot with butter, and it dries out before I finish it. Cornbread has become a dessert, a cake! Locally, I'm up against the cornbread at Hundred Acres and the Dutch, hot restaurants a block away. Both have made a light, sweetish chunk of cornbread the signature starch. Tasty. But that's a lot of white flour and sugar to eat before dinner. History, I see, is on my side. Jeremy Jackson, the author of *The Cornbread Book: A Love Story with Recipes,* says that Ozark cornbread—all cornmeal, no flour, no sugar—was the dish most Americans once ate. But even I'll admit that sounds a bit grim. So, to please the ones I love, here is an ethereal recipe from Hundred Acres, a wonderful American place on MacDougal Street. At least it calls for plenty of butter. I always use a cast-iron skillet. For a crustier crust, preheat the skillet.

¾ c (1 ½ sticks or 6 oz or 12 T) unsalted butter plus more for the pan

2 ¼ c coarse cornmeal

2 ¼ c all-purpose white flour

½ cup plus 2 T sugar

3 T Bob's Red Mill baking powder

2 tsp salt

4 eggs

1 ½ c milk

1. Set the oven to 350°F.
2. Butter a 10-inch cast iron skillet.
3. Start to melt the ¾ cup of butter in another pan.
4. Mix the dry ingredients thoroughly. Leave no baking powder lumps.
5. Whisk the eggs in another bowl and add the milk.
6. Slowly pour the wet mixture into the dry; mix well.
7. Add the melted butter and mix well.
8. Pour the batter into the skillet and bake for about 45 minutes, or until a knife in the center comes out clean. ✢

nina's cornbread

In place of the flour and sugar, use 2½ cups of coarse cornmeal, 1 cup of white flour, 1 cup of white whole wheat flour, and ¼ cup of unrefined cane sugar, maple syrup, or honey.

yogurt or buttermilk cornbread

Replace some or all of the milk with yogurt or buttermilk. You'll get that tangy tingle and give the baking powder a kick.

cornbread with creamed corn

Boil 3 ears of corn in salted water for 3 minutes. Slice off the kernels. Then scrape them with a knife to harvest all the pulp and milk you can. Add it to the wet ingredients.

hot pepper cornbread

Dice a jalapeño or cayenne pepper and sauté in olive oil until it's half-soft. Add to the wet ingredients.

pie crust

Makes two 8- to 10-inch pie crusts

My favorite way to eat the little wheat I eat is with lots of butter. Butter is what makes a shortbread cookie and a short crust pastry "short." Its hallmarks are flakiness, crumbs, and crevices—the little gaps left where the butter has melted. But short pastry takes practice. A light touch is required; the pastry is tough when overworked. If you don't have a food processor, cut the butter into the flour with a pastry cutter or two butter knives, working fast, as if you were sharpening them. For a sweet crust, add three tablespoons of sugar to the flour and salt. You can make a lard crust in just the same way, with one cup of lard, but I've had the best luck using mostly butter with a little lard, in a ratio of about two to one. Like the butter, the lard must be very cold; you can chill it in the fridge or freezer. The freezer is also the place to put the second crust—do not roll it out—if you are not making a double-crust pie today.

This is the crust for Lemon Curd Tart (p. 205), Honey Pumpkin Pie (p. 207), Butternut Squash Pie (p. 206)—or any filling you choose.

1 c (2 sticks or 8 oz or 16 T) unsalted butter
2 c all-purpose pastry flour
1 tsp unrefined sea salt
3 T organic whole cane sugar (optional)
¼-½ c ice water

1. Chill all the ingredients before you start.
2. Cut the cold butter into small pieces.
3. Put the flour, salt, and (optional) sugar in the food processor. Add the pieces of butter and chop the mixture for about 10 seconds, or just until it is evenly coarse. The pieces of butter should be lentil-sized.
4. Slowly add the ice water, drop by drop, down the tube with the machine running, just until the dough holds together—not more than 30 seconds. Test the dough by pinching it. If it's crumbly, add a bit more water.
5. Turn the dough onto a large piece of plastic wrap and flatten it into a thick disk, wrap it well, and refrigerate it for an hour. (You can do this much one day ahead.)
6. Split the chilled dough in half and make two disks. Put them on a floured surface or between sheets of parchment paper and use a rolling pin to flatten them, rolling from the center out.
7. If you need a fully baked crust for a chilled filling, such as Lemon Curd Tart, set the oven to 400°F. Lay the pastry in the pie pan, poke a few holes in the bottom with a fork, and cover it with foil and something heavy, like beans or another pie pan. Bake it for about 10 minutes, then remove the foil and bake it for another 5 minutes or more, until the crust is golden. ✢

easy pizza crust

Makes two 12-inch crusts

It really is easy. I've never had much luck with whole wheat baking, so this marks another instance of my dictum: a little white flour now and then won't hurt you. Molino Caputo makes a superior flour for the purpose called Tipo 00. The natural (not added) gluten makes the dough stretchy yet strong. Failing that, use King Arthur bread flour. You can refrigerate the dough in a lightly oiled freezer bag for one day, or wrap it tightly and freeze it for up to one month. Thaw and bring the dough to room temperature before shaping the crust. (Pizza stone users will follow specific baking instructions.) Some homemade and store-bought toppings to consider: Griddled Onions (page 139), Griddled Red Peppers (page 137), pitted kalamata olives, spicy salami, mozzarella, salted ricotta, and Fontina Fontal. Shaved Parmigiano-Reggiano is a fine way to top it all off.

8 oz warm water
1 tsp honey or organic whole cane sugar
1 T dry yeast
1 T olive oil
½ tsp unrefined sea salt
4 ½ c Molino Caputo Tipo 00 pizza flour
Simple Pizza Sauce recipe follows

1. Put the warm (not hot) water in a large bowl. Dissolve the honey or sugar fully, then add the yeast. Let the mixture stand until bubbly, about 5 to 15 minutes.
2. Add the oil, salt, and 4 cups of the flour. Form the mixture into a ball that pulls away from the sides of the bowl.
3. Flour the counter. Turn the dough out and knead it for a full five minutes (or longer) until it is firm, smooth, elastic, and not too sticky.
4. Put dough in a clean, lightly oiled bowl. Rub a bit of oil over the ball and cover it with a cloth. Leave it in a warm, draft-free spot until it has more than doubled in size, about 2 hours. (This is the time to prepare the pizza topping.)
5. When the dough has risen, set the oven to 500°F. Punch it down, divide it in half, and make two smooth balls. (Now you can refrigerate or freeze it.)
6. Lightly oil the pizza pan. Gently stretch and flatten the dough across the pan to spread it evenly, pressing it down as you go.
7. Dress the pizza with a thin layer of sauce, add the toppings, and bake for about 25 minutes, until the dough is golden brown and pulls away from the edges. ✢

simple pizza sauce

For the indispensable silky layer between the crust and the toppings, make this easy sauce. It will cover four pizzas. Use the rest to start a beefy red sauce for pasta, or freeze it for the next pizza night.

1 16-oz can good peeled tomatoes, such as San Marzano

¾ c olive oil

1 large bunch of basil—enough to yield about 1 c leaves

1 clove garlic

salt and pepper

Purée it all in the blender. Season to taste. Cover and refrigerate up to three days.

jim lahey's crusty bread

Serves 8

This no-knead, crusty dome from Jim Lahey, bread prodigy and founder of Sullivan Street Bakery, is the only yeast bread I understand (however meagerly), and it could make a baker out of any first-timer who still eats gluten. My friend Pam Flory, an organic farmer and real-food-in-schools activist, baked the first Jim Lahey loaf I ate, and one day she showed me how. Her loaf, made with one-third whole-wheat flour, was amazing. Sometimes she shapes it in a thick baguette and bakes it uncovered on a sheet, which yields a smaller slice and softer crust—nice for sandwiches. You'll need a covered pot made of cast iron (plain or enameled), oven-proof glass, or ceramic of 4, 6, or 8 quarts. I use a large ceramic Emile Henry Dutch oven. It's lighter than my everyday-use cast-iron and easier to lift in and out of the oven. Extravagantly, I keep it for bread only.

When I used my soup-and-everything-else pots, the hot oven burned off tiny amounts of garlic and who knows what, bits that don't belong on a clean pot but were there anyway. A tip from Pam: When you first mix the dough, you are not kneading, just incorporating. Get it done quickly, in two minutes or less. The secret is in the long rise. "Let the yeast do its job slowly," she says.

3 c King Arthur all-purpose or bread flour plus more for dusting

¼ tsp instant yeast

1 ¼ tsp salt

1 ⅓ c cold water

1. Mix the flour, yeast, and salt in a large bowl. Add the water and—working quickly—stir until they're blended; the dough will be shaggy and sticky. Cover with cloth. Let the dough rest 12 to 18 hours at room temperature, about 70°F degrees. Twenty-four hours is not too long.

2. The dough is ready when it's dotted with bubbles. Dust the counter with flour, lift the dough out in one piece, and put the dough down. Flour your hands. Sprinkle the dough with a little more flour and fold it over on itself a few times, gently and quickly forming an imperfect disk.

3. Coat a dish towel with flour. Put the dough seam-side down on the cloth and dust it again. Cover it with another towel and let it rise for 2 to 3 hours. When the dough has doubled in size and it doesn't spring right back when you poke it, it's ready.

4. About 30 minutes before the dough is ready to bake, set the oven to 475°F. Heat the pot and lid for about 30 minutes.

5. Carefully take the hot pot out of the oven. Gently turn the dough into the pot, seam-side up. It looks messy, but the seams will split and crack beautifully. Shake the pan a little to settle the dough.

6. Cover and bake for 30 minutes. Uncover and bake another 15 to 30 minutes, until the loaf is chestnut brown.

7. Cool on a rack for one hour. ✣

pam flory's bread

Serves 8 to 10

Pam uses Jim's method and makes a double recipe in a seven-quart Dutch oven. These are her proportions.

4 c King Arthur white all-purpose or bread flour

2 c King Arthur whole grain white wheat bread flour

3 tsp salt

2 tsp instant yeast

3 c cold water

sweets

Fruit Salad ÷ A Downy Vanilla Cheesecake

Panna Cotta ÷ Coeur à la Crème ÷ Butternut Squash Pie

Honey Pumpkin Pie ÷ Pumpkin Pie Custard

Lemon Curd ÷ Orange Custard ÷ Rosemary Shortbread

Chocolate Mousse ÷ Chocolate Bark

White Cow Dairy Custard ÷ Crème Anglaise

Oatmeal Peanut Butter Cookies

Peach Melba ÷ Stewed Prunes

Vanilla Bean Ice Cream ÷ Milk Chocolate Ice Cream

Crème Fraîche Custard Ice Cream

Anniversary Peaches & Cream Ice Cream

fruit salad

Rob does not eat fresh fruit. At first I considered this a flaw. On some days, I suppose I still do. Year-round there are bowls of fruit—local and seasonal, exotic and store-bought—on our counter. I eat it three times a day. What's his problem? Now I know. What Rob really likes is a nice fruit salad: uneven, chunky local peaches and blueberries jostling Costa Rican pineapple, all of it sloshing in a splash of fresh orange juice, which, after an hour or so, has magically quadrupled into a bath of off-pink mingled juices. The fruit salad Rob makes is always perfect, and I mention it here not because you need me to tell you how to make it, but to remind myself to make it more often.

a downy vanilla cheesecake

Serves 6 to 8

Intense and dense, or light and fluffy? Cheesecake partisans will never agree. But Rob dubbed this "A Cheesecake Jews and Italians Will Love." Ricotta makes it fluffy, crème fraîche makes it tangy, and cream cheese makes it silky. Better ingredients—in my kitchen, Vermont Butter and Cheese Creamery crème fraîche, Ben's Cream Cheese, small-batch ricotta, pastured eggs—will have them raving. Having agonized over an alternative to the graham-cracker crust, I've settled on no crust. Do spend a precious dollar on a real vanilla pod (or two) for the round, deep flavor of its paste. The freckly, speckly seeds also make a lovely pattern. The longer the paste infuses the crème fraîche, the better. Unrefined sugar lends a mild caramel color and flavor. I made this in 4-inch springform pans for Rose and Jacob's "Bye Bye Baba" party. Sometimes it's hard to say goodbye to the joys of infancy, so we had a party to bid farewell to breastfeeding.

1 or 2 vanilla beans (or 1 tsp vanilla extract)
1 ½ c crème fraîche (about 16 oz)
1 ½ c cream cheese (about 12 oz)
½ c fresh ricotta (about 8 oz)
½ c organic whole cane sugar
4 eggs

1. Bring the ingredients to room temperature.
2. Set the oven to 325°F.
3. Split the vanilla bean lengthwise and scrape the seeds into the crème fraîche. Put the pod in, mix, and set it aside.
4. Line the bottom of a 9-inch springform pan with parchment paper and set it on top of foil on a baking sheet. (Sometimes the pan leaks a little.)
5. With beaters or in a food processor, mix the cream cheese and ricotta until very smooth.
6. Take the vanilla pod out of the crème fraîche.
7. Add the crème fraîche, sugar, and eggs to the ricotta and cream cheese. Mix until smooth.
8. Pour the batter into the mold. Bake for 10 minutes at 325°F.
9. Lower the oven to 250°F and bake until the cake is just set, about 1 hour. The center will be slightly wobbly.
10. *The more gradually the cake cools, the less likely it will collapse.* Turn off the oven and open the door slightly. Wait about 15 minutes, and then open it wider and wait another 15 minutes. Now let the cake cool on the counter. It will pull away from the edges and may have a lovely jagged split.
11. Serve chilled or—my preference—at room temperature. ✚

panna cotta

Serves 6

Panna cotta, or "cooked cream," is a molded, chilled dessert. Silky and lightly sweetened, it's never too much after dinner. You can vary the proportions of cream and milk and the flavors ad libitum. I've made this modest Italian dessert with buttermilk and yogurt in place of some of the milk and cream, and with honey or maple syrup in place of the sugar. You can also make it with raw milk and call it *panna cruda*. Simmer the vanilla bean and sugar with just a bit of the unpasteurized milk. Remove it from the heat, add the gelatin, and mix well. Now add the rest of the raw milk. The unpasteurized milk stays raw, and it sets perfectly. Panna cotta is delicious with sweet cherries, peaches, or raspberries; I also like it with toasted pine nuts and a dribble of honey.

2 ½ c cream
½ c milk
4 T sugar (or up to ⅓ c)
1 vanilla bean
1 envelope unflavored gelatin (about 3 T)
2 T warm water

1. Mix the cream, milk, and sugar in a saucepan.
2. Split the vanilla bean lengthwise and scrape the paste into the cream mixture. Drop the pod in and warm until it simmers.
3. Remove the pan from the heat. Let the mixture rest and the flavors join. Overnight is not too long; if so, refrigerate it.
4. When you are ready to set the panna cotta, dissolve the gelatin in warm water.
5. Add the gelatin to the cream and mix well.
6. Pour it into ramekins. Chill it for at least 4 hours. The panna cotta should be like a soft jelly.
7. Carefully turn the panna cotta upside down onto a small dessert plate and gently ease off the ramekin. Garnish and serve at once. ✛

coeur à la crème

Serves 6

I have fiddled and fiddled with this French country dessert until it's just the way I like it, but cannot claim that the result is traditional. I doubt anyone could pin down a definitive recipe, because so many ingredients work well. Many fresh cheeses are used: *fromage frais,* English curd cheese, mascarpone, and ricotta. A drained, unbaked cheesecake, coeur à la crème is traditionally made in perforated, heart-shaped ceramic molds, and I confess that these lovely white dishes are one of the single-use toys I keep high on a shelf. They are so pretty! Heart-shaped or not, you must have a small, shallow perforated dish. Make the coeur à la crème the day before you serve it so that it has ample time to drain.

½ c good cream cheese, such as Ben's
1 T cream
1 vanilla bean
1 c crème fraîche
1 c ricotta cheese
2–3 T organic whole cane sugar
raspberry sauce (recipe follows), honey, or maple syrup to serve

1. Put the cream cheese and cream in the food processor and whip until it's creamy.
2. Split the vanilla bean lengthwise and scrape out the seeds and paste into the cream cheese. Add the crème fraîche, ricotta, and sugar. Whiz until it's smooth.
3. Line the heart-shaped molds with fine cheesecloth and spread the mixture in.
4. Set the hearts on a rack in a shallow pan. Cover the pan with plastic film or foil and refrigerate. Let the perforated dishes drain for one day.
5. Turn the little hearts out gently on a plate and drizzle with raspberry sauce, honey, or maple syrup. ✛

raspberry sauce

1 pint fresh raspberries
1 T sugar
1 Meyer lemon (optional)

Mash the berries and sugar in a bowl. Juice the lemon to yield 1 teaspoon. (I often skip the lemon juice.) Add the lemon juice to the berries and let them rest for an hour or so—or even overnight in the fridge. Strain through a cloth or fine sieve and serve at once.

secrets of the pumpkin family

In the fall, winter squashes are abundant at local markets. They typically come in just after frost, farmers pick them all by November, and they keep beautifully on the farm all winter, so you don't have to gorge on winter squashes as you would those fleeting, perishable crops. They're creamy, dense, sweet, rich in beta-carotene, and delicious with butter. Do add the butter; you need fats to absorb the beta-carotene, which your body then converts to usable, true vitamin A.

Which to eat? Not the ornamental pumpkins, which have large seed cavities, thin and stringy flesh, and little flavor. (Only the seeds are worth eating. Roast them first.) The general rule is that the winter squashes with deeply ribbed, star-shaped stems are less tasty for eating. Star-stemmed squashes include ornamental pumpkins, delicata, and acorn squash. To me, they are stringy and bland; hence all that brown sugar they need. Squashes with rounder, knobbly stems make better eating. These include buttercup (greenish-black, round and flat), Hubbard (the giant gray-blue one), and Japanese red kuri; most have creamy, dense flesh.

Notable exceptions to the stem rule are the flesh-colored squashes of the *Cucurbita moschata* species, including the butternut squash and the Long Island cheese pumpkin. Butternut has a long neck and a bulb at one end, while the cheese pumpkin is squat and round, like a wheel of Parmigiano. Though they sport the telltale skinny, ribbed stem, these are in fact the best eaters.

The pumpkin pie industry knows all this. In a tin of canned pumpkin, you'll find long-neck pumpkin, an ancestor of butternut squash, and when you see one, you'll know it straightaway. It looks just like a butternut, but with a very long, curved neck, and it can weigh up to twenty pounds. If you lug one home, you will be rewarded by a small seed cavity, smooth flesh, and excellent flavor. A popular nineteenth-century variety, Pennsylvania Dutch crookneck squash, is still found in many Amish gardens. You'll find it in heirloom seed catalogs.

Now you know the best way to make a pumpkin pie from local squash. Just buy, bake, and purée a butternut, long-neck, or cheese pumpkin. Hubbard and buttercup work, too—each with a slightly different flavor—but don't bother with "sugar" or "pie" pumpkins, or the lesser squashes. Perhaps they've improved, but I doubt it.

butternut squash pie

Serves 8

Butternut is a sister of pumpkin pie—not a twin—and makes a nice change in flavor. My taste runs to fluffy, rather than dense, squash pies; hence the generous number of eggs. The custard is a light orange and not too sweet. I love vanilla, but it's not traditional. Because custards should be smooth and silky, I use the food processor. If you mix by hand or with a handheld electric beater, whisk the eggs first. Then add all the other ingredients and mix again.

1 pie crust (page 187)

2 butternut squashes

2 T olive oil

4 eggs

½ c organic whole cane sugar

½ c milk

½ c cream

1 tsp vanilla (optional)

1 ½ tsp ground cinnamon

¼ tsp ground ginger

¼ tsp freshly ground nutmeg plus more for dusting

½ tsp salt

1 pt heavy cream for whipping (optional)

1. Make one 9-inch crust. Blind bake it at 400°F for 10 minutes. It will finish baking once you fill it. (You can do this one day ahead. Cover the crust with plastic wrap and refrigerate overnight.)
2. Set the oven to 350°F.
3. Wash and split the squashes in half lengthwise. Lightly oil the fleshy sides.
4. Lay the squashes cut-side down in a glass dish or iron skillet and bake until they are tender when poked.
5. Let the squash cool, remove the seeds and stringy bits, skin it, and purée it. Measure 2 cups of squash.
6. When you are ready to make the pie, set the oven to 400°F.
7. Put all the ingredients except the cream in the food processor and blend until the mixture is smooth.
8. Pour it into the pie crust. Cover the edge with foil to prevent too much browning.
9. Bake the pie for about 50 minutes or until a knife inserted in the center comes out clean. It should not be wobbly. Watch the crust. You'll probably take the foil off for the last 15 minutes to let it brown nicely. Cool the pie; if you're not serving it today, refrigerate it.
10. Serve the pie slightly chilled or at room temperature, with (optional) whipped cream and a grating of nutmeg. ✢

honey pumpkin pie

Serves 8

Though I've peeled and baked many a winter squash, I also consider it perfectly reasonable to buy canned organic pumpkin, and do so often. The same half cup of honey, maple syrup, or whole cane sugar works just fine in all the squash pies and custards here. I sometimes use a three-quarter cup, but one cup is too sweet for me.

1 pie crust (page 187)
4 eggs
1 15-oz (425-g) can organic pumpkin
½ c honey
½ c milk
½ c cream
1 tsp vanilla (optional)
1½ tsp ground cinnamon
½ tsp salt
¼ tsp ground ginger
¼ tsp freshly ground nutmeg plus more for dusting
1 pt heavy cream for whipping (optional)

1. First make one 9-inch crust. Blind bake it at 400°F for 10 minutes. It will finish baking once you fill it. (You can do this one day ahead. Cover the crust with plastic wrap and refrigerate overnight.)
2. Set the oven to 400°F.
3. Put all the ingredients except the cream in the food processor and blend until the mixture is completely smooth.
4. Pour it into the pastry crust. Cover the edge with tinfoil to prevent too much browning.
5. Bake the pie for about 50 minutes or until a knife inserted in the center comes out clean. It should not be wobbly. Watch the crust. You'll probably take the foil off for the last 15 minutes to let it brown nicely. Cool the pie; if you're not serving it today, refrigerate it.
6. Serve the pie slightly chilled or at room temperature, with whipped cream and a grating of nutmeg. ✛

pumpkin pie custard

Serves 8

This is the pumpkin dessert I make most often. Without a crust, it's no work at all, and the crust in the center of a pumpkin pie can get soggy. When you set a little dish of custard topped with whipped cream and a dusting of fresh nutmeg before each person, it makes a beautiful impression.

4 eggs

1 15-oz (425-g) can organic pumpkin

½ c maple syrup

½ c milk

½ c cream

1 tsp vanilla

1 ½ tsp ground cinnamon

¼ tsp ground ginger

¼ tsp freshly ground nutmeg plus more for dusting

½ tsp unrefined sea salt

1 pt heavy cream for whipping (optional)

1. Set the oven to 400°F.
2. Put all the ingredients except the cream in the food processor and blend until the mixture is completely smooth.
3. Pour into eight 4-ounce glass or ceramic ramekins.
4. Set the ramekins in a pan of water.
5. Bake the custards for about 30 minutes, until the tops are golden and the center is set. Remove them from the water bath and let them cool. If you are serving them the next day, cover the dishes with plastic wrap and refrigerate.
6. Serve the custard slightly chilled or at room temperature with (optional) whipped cream and a dusting of nutmeg. ✢

lemon curd

Makes 1 cup, which will fill an 8-inch tart shell or 4 little tart shells

Certain foodists are not kind about Martha Stewart. She's earnest, mainstream, and (we might guess) too successful. But I learned to cook—or began to—by reading *Quick Cook Menus: Fifty-two Meals You Can Make in Under an Hour* straight through at the age of nineteen. In her 1985 classic, *Pies and Tarts,* she did everything locavores do, but before it was cool. There's her vivid greenhouse spinach and herbs (in February), and there's the rich yellow lemon curd (made from her backyard chicken eggs) next to a paler version made with ordinary eggs. On the facing page, you see the difference. On the right I used pastured eggs, real butter, and a Meyer lemon, which adds nearly orange flecks of zest. Real food was always her style; and then, there was her *style.* Because of her obsession with eclectic fabrics, forks, and dishes, I started my modest Fiestaware collection with a few turquoise plates found at a flea market in Atlantic City. Martha Stewart's early books are notable for good taste in ingredients, recipes that work, and her own voice. I offer you her dense lemon curd, with a bit less sugar than the one cup she calls for. You are quite welcome to sweeten it further. Lemon curd is delicious on toast and biscuits. Or pour it into a prebaked pie crust (page 187).

3 Meyer lemons
⅔ c organic whole cane sugar
½ c (1 stick or 4 oz or 8 T) cold unsalted butter
6 egg yolks

1. Grate about 1 tablespoon of lemon zest with a zester or on the finest grater you have. Don't let the bitter white pith sneak in.
2. Squeeze the lemons to yield ½ cup of juice. Mix it with the sugar and zest.
3. Cut the butter in small pieces.
4. Separate the eggs and whisk the yolks. For a perfectly silky curd, strain the yolks through a sieve directly into a cold saucepan.
5. Add the sugar and lemon mixture to the saucepan and stir well. I usually set the pan in a water bath for extra security against overcooking. Cook over low heat, stirring constantly, for 10 to 12 minutes, until the liquid coats a wooden spoon.
6. Take the pan off the heat and mix until the mixture cools slightly.
7. Add the butter, one piece at a time, until it's fully incorporated.
8. Let it cool completely. ✢

orange custard

Makes twelve 4-ounce custards

When it's time for sweets, I am a sucker for milk and eggs, and I love all citrus. This is Michele Pulaski's orange custard, a delicate, silky thing that she has served at many elegant parties and that I could eat every day. I've reduced the sugar so you can taste plenty of orange and eat it with impunity, but sweetness is yours to tweak. Our small children love it. You'll need a large tray and a dozen 4-ounce ramekins.

2 oranges

8 eggs

½ c sugar

3 c cream

1 c milk

1. Set the oven to 300°F and prepare a water bath for the ramekins. I use a large baking tray and put about 2 inches of water in it. Test it first, to make sure the ramekins won't float away and the water won't spill.
2. Grate the orange rinds with a zester or with the smallest grater you have.
3. Separate six eggs. Set aside the whites for another use. Whisk two whole eggs with the six yolks.
4. Whisk the sugar into the eggs.
5. Gently heat the cream and milk with the orange zest. Let it cool. If it is too warm, the eggs will cook when you add them.
6. Add the egg mixture to the milk, a little bit at a time, whisking as you do.
7. Pour the custard into 4-ounce ramekins, filling them equally.
8. Place the custards in the water-bath tray and gently slide it into the oven. Bake them for about 50 minutes or until the custard sets. The center will be slightly soft.
9. Remove the ramekins from the water and cool. Cover with plastic wrap and refrigerate.
10. Serve chilled. ✢

rosemary shortbread

Serves 8

Melissa Clark wrote this recipe for a flexible shortbread. It was Christmas, and she called for rosemary, a savory flavor I happen to love, but anything goes: orange zest, honey instead of sugar. You must be terribly careful with the food processor. A moment too long and the dough will be overdone, and your shortbread, though delicious, will crumble at the touch. It's nice if some squares come out neatly.

2 c white flour
⅔ c organic whole cane sugar
1 T fresh rosemary, finely chopped
1 tsp unrefined sea salt
1-2 tsp dark, rich honey
1 c (2 sticks or 8 oz or 16 T) unsalted cold butter

1. Set the oven to 325°F.
2. In a food processor, pulse the flour, sugar, rosemary, and salt. Drop the honey in.
3. Take the cold butter out of the fridge and cut it in chunks. Put them in the food processor and pulse to fine crumbs. Be restrained! The dough should not be smooth.
4. Press the dough into an ungreased 8- or 9-inch square baking dish. Prick the dough all over with a fork.
5. Bake until it's golden brown, about 35 minutes.
6. Cut the shortbread in squares while it's still warm and thus a little pliable. ✣

Plain

Omit the rosemary and honey.

Vanilla

Make plain shortbread. Add 2 teaspoons of vanilla extract with the butter or scrape the seeds and paste of a vanilla bean into the flour mixture.

Not So Sweet

Use ⅓ c of sugar.

Honey

Replace the sugar with ⅓ c of honey.

Citrus

Add 1 to 1 ½ teaspoons of lemon zest or orange zest with the flour.

Maple Nut

Grind ½ cup of lightly toasted walnuts or almonds with the flour and replace the sugar with maple sugar.

chocolate mousse

Serves 8 to 10

My version of the classic chocolate mousse in *Bistro Cooking* by Patricia Wells is more dense than fluffy. I always use a 70% eating chocolate because that is what we have in the cupboard, because it's better than most baking chocolate, and because it's easy to measure and to melt. (I hate to weigh things.) If you use unsweetened chocolate, double the sugar. The whipped cream and chocolate garnish are discretionary.

8 eggs

2 bars (200 g or 7 oz) 70% chocolate

½ c (1 stick or 4 oz or 8 T) butter

2 tsp vanilla extract

pinch of salt

¼ c organic whole cane sugar

3 c heavy cream to serve

piece of chocolate, cacao nibs, or chocolate twigs to serve

1. Separate the eggs, being sure to keep every bit of yolk out of the whites. Set the whites aside. In a large glass bowl, whisk the yolks well.
2. Break up the chocolate and cut up the butter.
3. In a bowl over a pan of boiling water, gently melt the chocolate, butter, and vanilla. Remove the pan from the heat.
4. Put the egg whites in a large clean bowl. Add the salt and beat until they are half-stiff. Then add the sugar and beat them until you see shiny peaks.
5. Add the warm chocolate to the egg yolks—not the reverse—while whisking continuously.
6. Add a third of the egg whites to the chocolate and mix thoroughly. Gently fold in the rest of the egg whites to make the mousse fluffy. Do not overmix it, but don't leave any egg-white streaks either.
7. Pour the mousse into a glass serving bowl or spoon it into individual dishes. Cover each dish with plastic wrap and chill for at least 3 hours or overnight.
8. When you're ready to serve the mousse, whip the cream. Shave a little chocolate with a grater or vegetable peeler. (If the kitchen is hot, chill the chocolate bar first.) Put a dollop of cream on each serving and sprinkle the chocolate on top. ✣

chocolate bark

Serves 4 to 6

It's easy to unwrap a bar of chocolate after dinner, but if you'd like something a little special, try this.
Play with the flavors—try cinnamon, nutmeg, or cayenne. Wrapped in parchment paper and tied with a ribbon, chocolate bark makes a lovely gift.

½ c walnuts, pecans, almonds, or other nuts

2 bars (200 g or 7 oz) 70% chocolate

½ c dried cranberries or cherries, candied citrus peel, or other dried fruit

1. Set the oven to 300°F.
2. Toast the nuts in the oven for 8 to 10 minutes, or use a dry skillet and turn the nuts constantly. Do not burn. Chop the nuts roughly.
3. Break up the chocolate in a glass or stainless steel bowl. Set the bowl in a pan of boiling water and melt it over moderate heat. Stir the chocolate and scrape down the sides. When it's creamy, take it off the heat.
4. Lay parchment paper on a flat sheet and spread the mixture over it. Sprinkle the nuts and fruit on top of the chocolate while it's still sticky.
5. Chill the bark it until it's firm. Break it in pieces. Keep it in the fridge in an airtight container. ✣

handmade, hill country foods

In the summer of 2006 I was pregnant with Julian. I also went on a book tour for *Real Food: What to Eat and Why* and opened two experimental Real Food Markets in New York. Too ambitious. Something had to give, and so I let the markets close after one season. But at least one gem, a milky, opalescent gem, came out of my little enterprise. I found White Cow Dairy, founded by Patrick Lango, a fast-talking chef and fourth-generation dairy farmer in East Otto, New York, south of my native Buffalo. The notes from our first conversation about his little creamery include the words "genius" and "crazy." The adjectives were mine, but Patrick would agree. His custards, yogurts, and cultured creams I understood, but plans for a grass-fed whey "sports drink" sounded peculiar. For a while, Patrick would send us small glass jars of dairy treats packed in ice. Baby Julian and I gobbled them up. When a similar package appeared at Murray's Cheese, Rob wrote, "Nothing has ever walked in the door like the fresh dairy that arrived from your farm this morning! Who are you, where are you, and where in the world did you learn to make foods like these?"

I was wrong about Patrick's wacky whey drinks, which are tangy, delicious, unlike any other drink, and now bought in bulk by fanatics from Buffalo to New York City. Patrick insists that the magic of his foods comes not from his skill, but from the grass and hay in his pastures. "Great ingredients make great food," he says. Which is very sound-bitey of my friend Patrick, who is more a poet of the romantic transcendentalist school. "The sun, soils, and flora of the old-time hills are overrun with coltsfoot, beebread, burdock, violet, fescue, buttercup, birdsfoot, chamomile, peppermint, chickweed, wild strawberry, yarrow, horehound, yellowdock, feltwort, orchard grass, nettles, and clover," he writes. The milk from this diet of grasses, flowers, and weeds yields subtle mineral distinctions to each batch of handmade foods.

In a world of mass-made, dairylike foods made of crushed soybeans, what Patrick does is extraordinary, though he doesn't see it that way:

we're lucky the foods are so good
we don't consider what we're doing to be anything out of the ordinary
it used to be, farmers made foods like ours everywhere
we'd like to see that again
and we're going to do our best
to make that happen

white cow dairy custard

Serves 8

An early tagline on White Cow Dairy's custard read, "iron, calcium, protein, pleasure." Patrick's custard is inspired by a recipe in *The Gold Cook Book* by Louis P. de Gouy, who noted that this delicate food nourished the young, the old, and especially the infirm; the dish was commonly served in nineteenth-century sanatoriums. Lucky invalids.

Since I started baking this custard, Patrick has given the basic vanilla two more notes by adding toasted coriander and French brandy. Now I keep a small jar of brandy in the fridge with a couple of vanilla beans in it. The coriander and nutmeg are quite bold, especially with whole, fresh spices. For a milder custard, feel free to experiment with just a whisper of the spices. Call it a dessert or a snack—it doesn't matter. It is the sort of dish I permit freely at all hours. If you don't have eight 8-ounce (one-cup) ramekins, use a shallow 9-by-12-inch glass baking dish.

1 tsp whole coriander seeds

1 split vanilla bean, soaked in Armagnac

1 qt (4 c) milk

¼ c organic whole cane sugar (or maple sugar, maple syrup, or honey)

1 tsp chunky unrefined sea salt, such as Maldon or Jacobsen

8 eggs

1 nutmeg

1. Set the oven to 350°F.
2. In a dry pan, toast the coriander seeds gently and remove them from the pan. When they are cool, grind them into a rough powder with a mortar and pestle or the back of a spoon.
3. Scrape the vanilla seeds into the milk. Add the vanilla bean and ground coriander and heat gently. Let it cool a bit.
4. Stir in the sugar and salt.
5. Whisk the eggs so they are foamy but not stiff. Add the eggs to the milk and mix.
6. Grate a bit of nutmeg into the eight 8-ounce ramekins and pour the custard mix in slowly.
7. Set the ramekins in a pan of quite hot (not boiling) water.
8. Bake for 40 to 45 minutes or until the center is set and a knife slips out clean. ✢

crème anglaise

Serves 6 to 8

Crème anglaise—"English cream"—is a thin, pourable custard sauce made with milk or milk and cream. Country bumpkin that I was, I'd never seen it until moving to England, where it's beloved and often called custard. As with all stove-top custards, the trick is not to curdle it. This is also the moment to use the vanilla sugar you have cleverly made weeks before. (Split a vanilla bean and bury it in a jar of sugar.) Pour crème anglaise over berries, gingerbread, carrot cake, apple pie, or Apple Crisp (page 174).

1 c milk
1 c cream
1 vanilla bean
5 eggs
6 T organic whole cane sugar

1. Put the milk and cream in a pan. Split the vanilla bean, scrape the seeds into the milk, and then add the pod.
2. Heat the milk gently, just short of simmering. Take it off the heat and let it cool. Ideally, let it rest for 30 minutes to infuse the milk thoroughly with vanilla. (The more you get out of these pricey beans, the better.)
3. Separate the eggs and save the whites for another use.
4. In a bowl or pan you can set over a water bath, whisk the yolks with the sugar until smooth.
5. Set the pan of eggs over a simmering water bath. Slowly, and in small batches, pour the warm (not hot) milk into the eggs, mixing well each time.
6. Reheat the custard gently, whisking constantly and occasionally scraping the sides, until it thickens. In about 20 minutes, it will coat the back of a wooden spoon.
7. Take it off the heat and pour it into a bowl to cool, stirring it a few more times; otherwise the custard will overcook. You can also set the bowl in a cool water bath.
8. Serve warm or cool, in a bowl with a small ladle or in a little pitcher. ✢

oatmeal peanut butter cookies

Makes 4 dozen cookies

Martha Wilkie's cookie is perfect for children and grown-ups alike. Suit your sweet tooth and add more sugar for special occasions, but Martha's idea was an everyday cookie—not so sweet that her son, Petey, couldn't eat one at snack time. Muscovado is an unrefined brown sugar with a strong molasses flavor. It's a bit darker than most brown sugars, slightly moist, and easy to find. Look for real peanut butter: just peanuts and salt (photo on page 192).

3 c whole rolled oats

⅓ c King Arthur white whole wheat flour

1 tsp baking soda

1 tsp Bob's Red Mill baking powder

½ tsp unrefined sea salt

½ c muscovado sugar

½ c brown sugar

1 c coconut oil

½ c peanut butter

2 eggs

1 tsp vanilla

1 bar (100 g or 3.5 oz) 70% chocolate (optional)

2 c salted whole peanuts (optional)

1. Set the oven to 350°F.

2. Stir the oats, flour, baking soda, baking powder, and salt in a medium bowl. Set aside.

3. Put the sugars, oil, and peanut butter in a bowl and mix with an electric mixer on medium speed until well blended, about 5 minutes.

4. Mix in the eggs and vanilla.

5. Add the oat mixture, and mix until just combined.

6. Break up the (optional) chocolate into chunks. Add the chocolate and (optional) peanuts.

7. Drop balls of dough 2 inches apart on baking sheets.

8. Bake the cookies until they are golden brown, about 12 to 15 minutes, rotating the sheets halfway through. Let the sheets cool on wire racks for 5 minutes, then lift the cookies off the sheets and set them directly on the racks to cool completely.

9. Cookies can be stored in airtight containers at room temperature for up to 2 days or frozen for 3 months. ✣

peach melba

Serves 4

An unimpeachable high-summer dessert, peach melba was first created in 1892 by Auguste Escoffier in honor of Dame Nellie Melba, the Australian soprano. We served peach melba at our wedding, despite Rob's efforts to talk me into a traditional cake; I can be stubborn, and although it was delicious, I regretted it. While oblivious guests danced, the velvety August night melted the ice cream in many bowls. (I was sensibly seated, enjoying every bite.) In hindsight I would choose my own Downy Vanilla Cheesecake (page 195), made a touch sweeter for the special occasion. But I'm still glad we sidestepped the goofy moment where the happy couple feed each other in front of a hundred people.

1 pt raspberries
1 T sugar
1 Meyer lemon
4 ripe peaches
4 scoops Vanilla Bean Ice Cream (page 220)
handful of flaked almonds
4 butter cookies

1. Mash the berries and sugar in a bowl. Juice the lemon to yield 1 teaspoon. Add the lemon juice to the berries and let them rest at least 1 hour or overnight in the fridge. Strain through a cloth or fine sieve.
2. Boil water. Dip the whole peaches in the boiling water for 1 minute. Remove them with a slotted spoon. Peel, pit, and halve the peaches.
3. Set the peaches in dessert bowls or glasses. Add the ice cream and pour the raspberry sauce over it. Top with the almonds and tuck in a cookie. ✢

stewed prunes

Serves 2 to 4

Now, this is a dish I did not grow up on and would never have made in a million years had Rob not asked for it. Thankfully it seems there is no über-version in his variegated memory of his mother's cooking, so I've been able to make it just exactly my way, and to my surprise, I like stewed prunes quite a lot. I eat them plain or with crème fraîche or yogurt. Once, I gave Michele Pulaski some exquisite boiled apple cider syrup because she is like the sort of woman who looks great in fine jewels and ought to get them somehow, somewhere. Hanging out in her kitchen with her painter-roofer husband, Rye, and their sculptor-carpenter–nouveau hippie friends, I saw her dribble the syrup over a big green salad. Later I found myself at home with a large bowl of spinach and nothing sweet to counter the blue cheese and walnuts. Only dry vinegars; no ripe pears. But wait—in the fridge, a bowl of cider-stewed prunes. I dressed the salad first with olive oil (to coat the leaves) and then a sprinkling of the syrup. Prunes are spicy, yes, but so are red wine and balsamic vinegars.

1 c dried prunes
1 c unpasteurized orange juice or cider
1 cinnamon stick
crème fraîche or yogurt (for serving)

1. Soak the prunes in 1 cup of water for 6 to 12 hours. Overnight doesn't hurt.
2. Drain the prunes and simmer them in the orange juice or cider with the cinnamon stick until they are soft, 10 to 20 minutes.
3. When you have a nice syrup, the prunes are ready.
4. Serve with crème fraîche or yogurt. ✛

ice creams

Let's be candid. My ice cream doesn't taste, look, or feel like industrial ice cream—and it's not even as good as the small-batch, local ice cream we buy from Half Pint Kitchen, in Stockton, New Jersey—but it's fresh, it's delicious, it's fun to make, and it's a summer pastime in itself. It's all worth it when Julian tells his four-year-old friend, "We can't have ice cream *tonight*, William. Mommy has to *make* it." Organic whole cane sugar is one reason it's different. Whole sugar makes a vanilla ice cream the color of pale coffee, with a mild (and lovely) flavor of caramel. It has a similar, but more subtle, effect with chocolate and fruit flavors, so I choose flavors it flatters. Pure white sugar will give the ice cream pure color (as you see opposite) and pure sweetness, which is also nice and would suit certain flavors (such as lemon) better.

These ice creams are subtle on sweetness. If my recipes are not sweet enough for you, adding more sugar, maple syrup, or honey is easy: taste the batter, and add it before chilling. If you are using precious raw milk and cream, make the infusion (of vanilla beans or other flavors) with a small amount of cream. Chill the infusion, and then add the rest of the cold raw milk and cream to the chilled mix.

I still remember hot days in the front yard in Wheatland, Virginia, hand-cranking ice cream in a wooden bucket. Or one hot day, anyway. Lots of ice, lots of work, one great memory. And one memory is just enough. An electric ice cream churn is a luxury, a convenience, and an expensive, single-use tool, but I'm no martyr. Both kinds of electric ice cream churns are brilliant inventions. My fancy self-cooling number, by De'Longhi, delivers a beautiful texture and lets you make one batch after another without stopping to freeze the bowl, but it's expensive. The less pricey kind has a removable bucket that you must freeze at least one day in advance (and refreeze for each batch) and the texture of the ice cream is . . . homemade. Still, I've made all these ice creams in the latter kind, the affordable and unromantically named Cuisinart ICE series, and scores of eaters, young and old, devoured them happily.

If you use the removable-bucket type, a few tips will yield a better ice cream. Get the dasher going before you pour in the batter. Scrape it down with a rubber spatula a few times while it churns. Don't overfill it; this allows it to froth up without spilling over, adding more air. Pack the ice cream in cardboard pints (not quarts) so it freezes faster and more evenly. Serve it within two days. Let it soften in the fridge before scooping. When you pack the pints, put a piece of plastic film on top of the ice cream, and then put the lid on. These recipes make about one quart of ice cream, which easily serves our family of five—and often a guest or two—and happens to be the maximum my machine holds. The recipes are easily doubled.

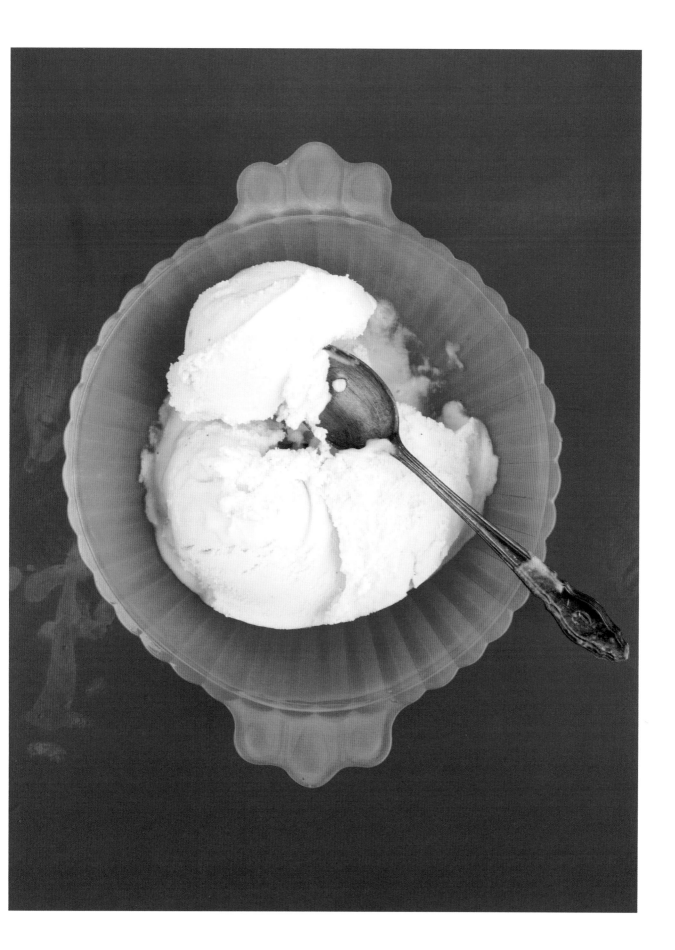

vanilla bean ice cream

Makes about 1 quart

I've tinkered plenty with the milk, cream, and sugar proportions for my House Vanilla and settled on this. For everyday home eating, I never use the full cup of sugar, but you might prefer it. If, like me, you love the intense flavor of honey and maple syrup, the right amount is one half cup (of either) in place of the sugar. My aim is an ice cream we can eat all summer, without breaking the sugar bank or going to bed too full of cream. Variations are child's play.

2 c cream

1 c milk

2 vanilla beans

⅔–1 c organic whole cane sugar or organic white sugar

1. Pour the cream and milk into a pan. Split the vanilla pods and scrape the tiny seeds into the milk. Add the pods and sugar to the milk. Mix well and heat gently, but do not boil.
2. Let it cool to room temperature.
3. Chill thoroughly in the refrigerator for up to 2 days.
4. Remove the pods and churn in your ice cream maker as instructed. ✛

Salted Vanilla Bourbon Pecan

The nuts and the spirits give the caramel quality of whole cane sugar the extra depth it craves. Soak the vanilla beans in bourbon or Armagnac. (I keep a small jar of spirits in the fridge with a couple of pods in it.) Slice and scrape the vanilla beans as usual. Add one teaspoon of the infused booze to the milk and cream. Near the end of the churning, when the ice cream is surging up in little waves, add a handful of pecans (or walnuts) and a sprinkling of coarse-ground unrefined sea salt. ✛

A Double Batch of Lighter Vanilla

4 c cream

4 c milk

3 vanilla beans

1 ⅓ c organic whole cane sugar

This is a slightly lighter (and larger) recipe using equal parts milk and cream. I like this texture as much as my House Vanilla, opposite page, but any combination of milk and cream is fair game. There's no extra work in making a larger batch; it's the same stirring. If your churn (like mine) does not hold a double batch, simply put half the mixture in the fridge. It only benefits from infusing overnight. Churn the other half and pack it in tubs today, refreeze the bucket overnight, and churn the other half tomorrow. With a double batch, you also have the chance to flavor one half and not the other. My favorite simple flavors are pecans, coarse sea salt, sweet black cherries packed in syrup, and chunks of good broken-up chocolate. Drop them in about halfway through the churning.

milk chocolate ice cream

Makes about 1 quart

In chocolate bars, I like austerity, and in chocolate mousse, intensity, but with ice cream the effect I want is akin to cold chocolate milk: in a word, milky. There may be more decadent chocolate ice creams, and there are certainly more complicated ones, but this is exactly what I'm looking for: it calls for simple ingredients I always have on hand, and it's terribly simple.

2 c cream
1 c milk
1 T organic whole cane sugar
1 bar (100 g or 3.5 oz) 70% chocolate

1. Put the cream, milk, and sugar in a pan. Mix well and heat gently.
2. Break up the chocolate, drop it in the milk, and melt it completely, mixing well.
3. Chill thoroughly. Mix it once more before you churn it; the chocolate sometimes settles.
4. Churn it in your machine as instructed. ✣

crème fraîche custard ice cream

Makes about 1 quart

Here is a more decadent ice cream, a frozen custard made with eggs. To the custard base, I've added a velvety cushion of crème fraîche, the butterfat-laden delicacy that used to be the little-known secret weapon of French cooks. The one we buy comes from one of the best American producers, the Vermont Butter and Cheese Creamery. It is not sour cream, but I've yet to learn how they are different. Both are cultured creams; if there is an American-milk sour cream made to the high standards of this crème fraîche, I'd like to try it.

3 egg yolks
¾ c sugar
1 ½ c cream
1 vanilla bean
1 c (8 oz) cold crème fraîche

1. Whisk the egg yolks and sugar.
2. Set a saucepan over a water bath and pour the cream into the pan. Split the vanilla pod and scrape the tiny seeds into the cream. Add the pod. Heat gently, but do not boil.
3. Cool slightly and whisk in the egg-sugar mixture, stirring constantly, over very low heat.
4. Allow it to cool to room temperature.
5. Whisk in the crème fraîche. Chill thoroughly.
6. Remove the vanilla pod and churn the ice cream in your machine as instructed. ✣

anniversary peaches & cream ice cream

Makes about 1 quart

At our August wedding, there were many bowls and baskets of fresh, ripe peaches. They were as pretty as the local flower arrangements, but of course no one touched them, so we ate peaches for days. Nuptials or not, in late summer our house is peach-laden; we buy them two or three times a week, and Julian likes to eat four in a row. I hide them on a high shelf until they are ripe and put a few ripe ones on the butcher block each morning. My new tradition is making peach ice cream, the very model of a homemade summer treat, on our anniversary, or thereabouts.

This one is more cream than peach; for a more intense fruit flavor, use six peaches, and cook them down more. Note: there are no frozen peach chunks here. I don't like the iciness. Nor is it pink. It's flesh colored; that is, if you have the flesh of a three-year-old child of European-American descent who has been running around naked catching chickens.

4 large ripe peaches
½ c organic whole cane sugar
2 c cream
½ c milk
1 vanilla bean
salt

1. Peel the peaches. Cut the flesh in chunks. Put the fruit in a pan with the sugar and a splash of water. Cook over low heat until they are soft, about 10 minutes.
2. Meanwhile, pour the cream and milk into another pan.
3. Split the vanilla bean. Scrape the paste into the cream and toss in the pod. Warm the milk and cream gently to infuse it with vanilla. Don't let it boil.
4. Mix the peaches and cream, add a sprinkle of salt, and allow it to cool.
5. Remove the pod and purée the mixture until it's completely smooth. Chill it thoroughly in the fridge, ideally overnight.
6. Churn it in your machine as instructed. ✢

PECORINO ROMANO

NEPI, LAZIO, ITALY

Part of the daily rations for Roman legionaries in the 1st century AD. It is still traditionally made from pasteurized sheep's milk in the Roman countryside and is less hard and dry than its Sardinian-made counterparts. No need to ration, we have enough for you

$12⁹⁹ lb

the cheese board

Cheese Board with Drinks

Picnic of American Cheeses and Meats

The Cheese Course

our way with cheeses

We are not very organized about cheese. We eat the world's ten greatest and most famous cheeses more often than the ten latest award-winning small-batch cheeses (as good as they are), and we seldom plan a cheese board. And yet things work out. I ask about new cheeses, or Rob brings one home, just often enough to avoid being a cheese Luddite, and there's usually something in the fridge to top a chef salad or to make Rob's famous browned cheesy omelet. When Roy Gumpel, the photographer who shot the cover of Rob's new country album, *Sweet Virginia Girl*, came to Small Farm for the day, we found ourselves at the pool in the late afternoon and suddenly hungry. Just as suddenly I was self-conscious that I hadn't thought of anything to offer him before his long drive home. But a few minutes of rummaging in the kitchen produced some prosciutto, Mahón (a semi-firm Spanish cow cheese), local melon, tomatoes, wine, and iced coffee. Julian and Jacob wandered over and ate with us. Ah, for the days of three- and one-year-olds who will eat anything.

cheese board with drinks

Though simplicity itself, the cheese board intimidated me quite a bit. There's no need for you to fret. Tradition calls for an odd number of cheeses; we typically put out three, at most five. Buy cheese you like. If they're new to you, ask to taste them in the shop. Arrange the cheeses in a clockwise pattern on the plate, starting with the mildest and finishing with the most assertive flavor. It doesn't matter which cheese sits at twelve noon; eaters will be looking at your cheese board from all directions. The mildest cheese is often a fresh chèvre or a creamy soft-ripened number, and the most assertive is usually a sturdy washed-rind or a blue. Mix up the milks: goat, cow, sheep. Cut a few portions to get the party started; pressed cheeses should be in nice triangular wedges, but some cheddars make nice uneven chunks. One knife for each cheese is ideal, but there's no need to go chasing after special items. For drinks, I serve nuts or dried fruit and crusty bread. I prefer to save the moist condiments, whether sweet or sharp, such as honey or mostarda, for dessert plates, but anything goes. Oh yes, one other tip. When I first started to set out cheese for parties, I dutifully studied the cheeses beforehand, because friends always ask what they're eating and I am a new student of cheese. Imagine my relief when Rob stuck (as in "glued") the luscious descriptions on the label right on the slate next to the cheeses. He'd rather people answer their own questions about whether it's raw-milk or not, sheep or cow, from Wisconsin or Spain, the better to enjoy his own party.

Vermont Butter and Cheese Creamery Coupole

A decadent dome of fresh goat milk with an assertive rind and a fresh, milky center. The wrinkly, coral-like rind is just gorgeous—and edible.

Consider Bardwell Rupert

An aged, raw-milk Jersey cow cheese made in the Alpine style of Gruyère and Comté, with smooth, buttery flesh, the right sharpness, and hints of tropical fruit.

Old Chatham Kinderhook Creek

A pure sheep milk cheese from East Friesian ewes grazing on Hudson Valley pastures, this creamy recipe has a mushroomy touch at its peak.

picnic of american cheeses & meats

Rob will tell you, cheerfully, that Murray's once sold cured meats that were not very different from supermarket brands. Exactly the same cured meats, actually. But little by little he brought the salumi, charcuterie, sausages, and (yes) hot dogs up to the standards of the four hundred cheeses in the glass case. Now you can find all kinds of small-batch, artisanal, handmade, and slow American and European meats at Murray's Cheese. Christiano Creminelli, whose family "has been producing artisan meats as far back as the oldest aunt can remember"—makes Salame al Barolo, sopressata, prosciutto and prosciutto cotto, coppa, lardo, and other traditional Italian recipes stateside with organic and natural American meats. Another traditional maker on American soil is La Quercia—meaning "the oak," a traditional food for fine pigs and symbol of the province of Parma, Italy, where founders Herb and Kathy Eckhouse lived, love, and learned Parma ham. Surryano is fine Virginia ham, made from rare Six-Spotted Berkshire hogs raised on pasture. Smoked over hickory logs for a week and aged for more than a year, the mahogany ham rivals the best Serrano. Nothing is easier than meat and cheese for a picnic. Just remember the bread and butter, perhaps some pickles, and something tart to drink, like lemonade. A little lard goes a long way.

Creminelli Salumi Barolo (left)
La Quercia Coppa (center)
Surryano Ham (right)

Spring Brook Tarentaise
A raw-milk cheese with pineapple tones from grass-fed cows at
Thistle Hill Farm in Vermont (left)

Dante
A sharp, nutty seasonal sheep cheese made by Cedar Grove Cheese
in Plain, Wisconsin (center)

Pawlet
A buttery, washed-rind, raw-milk cheese made from Jersey cow milk
by Consider Bardwell in Vermont (right)

the cheese course

Once I thought a gargantuan appetite was required to eat cheese after dinner. Not so; it's just a nibble. The two critical elements of a great cheese course are careful selection and minimalism—one ounce of each cheese per person. In a good restaurant, you are in the hands of a curator of flavor. Let the chef de fromage do the work. Alternatively, do it for your friends. Choose three cheeses, five at most. Vary the milk: goat, cow, sheep. Vary the texture: firm, creamy, crumbly. Match each one with a small, tasty morsel: nuts, jam, membrillo, chocolate. I'm partial to the bitterness of walnuts, the leathery sweetness of apricots, and the cool crunch of apples. Curation done, turn to theatrics. For the best effect, cut each cheese for each guest and place the matching morsels next to it, rather than passing a platter.

At our wedding, we served a plate of Green Hill, an unctuous cow milk and cream bloomy-rind from Georgia; Spring Brook Tarentaise, a caramelly, raw Jersey-cow cheese from Vermont; and Chiriboga—one of my very favorite blues, in a crowded class—made in Bavaria by Arturo Chiriboga, an Ecuadorian who learned cheese in France. Feel free to duplicate our wedding cheese at any party; two years later, as I write, I'm still enchanted with these cheeses and want you to fall for them, too. Or try the matches below. Essence, an ice wine made with cider apples, has become my favorite wine with an after-dinner cheese course. Made in New Hampshire, it suggests honey, apricot jam, and of course, cider. It's smooth, yet lively and tart.

Little Big Apple
A bloomy-rind triple cream wrapped in brandy-soaked apple-tree leaves,
with Solebury Orchard apples

Prairie Breeze Cheddar
An Amish-country cheese both nutty and grassy, with a piece of Brooklyn-made
Mast Brothers hazelnut chocolate

Chiriboga Blue
A cow milk-and-cream, funky German blue, with walnuts

THE PANTRY
THE BARE MINIMUM ON
A FEW ESSENTIALS

When I Say "Salt": A Short Note on Ingredients

Unless I note otherwise, salt means unrefined sea salt and black pepper is freshly ground, nutmeg freshly grated. Herbs are always fresh, and parsley is flat-leafed. Butter is unsalted. Milk, yogurt, and sour cream are full-fat. I use organic whole cane sugar (evaporated cane juice), Grade B maple syrup (a bit darker than Grade A), and raw, unfiltered honey. I call for Meyer lemons (sweeter juice, less acid, a floral flavor, and a softer, thinner peel than typical lemons) in desserts and drinks, and ordinary lemons in savory dishes. For more, see each ingredient below.

Beef.

Grass-fed and local is best, but watch out: your farmer may or may not have a great butcher. Happily, some new butchers (Dickson's Farmstand Meats and Fleisher's) and some veterans (Golden Gate Meat Company) are bringing great meat and great butchery skills back together. It's no sin if the beef is finished on a little grain. This country's legendary grass farmer, Joel Salatin, once told me, "Even a wild cow would've eaten some seed heads in the fall."

Chicken.

Chickens are omnivores, and they cannot live on grass alone; they need protein, calcium from oyster shell, corn, bugs. Left free to forage on grass and under shrubbery, they love weeds and the bugs they find in them. This is called a "pastured" chicken and there is no substitute. It flesh is not wet or flabby and the flavor is superior.

Seafood.

Wild seafood, from sustainable fisheries, is usually best. It's clean and clean-tasting; it's firm, not flabby. Organic farmed salmon from Northern Europe is improving, but with wild Alaskan salmon within reach, I don't bother. One delicious exception: farmed freshwater trout from a farmer who is careful about clean water. Most commercial shrimp causes ecological devastation (in mangrove swamps, for example). Try wild Alaskan spot prawns instead. I'm lucky to live near waters roamed by independent fishermen who bring fresh ocean fish to Greenmarkets; no fishmonger in the city can compare.

Eggs.

The eggs of a pastured laying hen can be called "pastured"—and once again, there is no substitute. They are rich yellow, with more omega-3 fats and vitamin E than eggs from chickens who never go outside. I don't buy eggs from hens whose diet is enhanced with fish oil, but the yolks do show more omega-3 fats. That said, the egg is a perfect food, and I would serve cheap eggs if cheap eggs were all I could find or afford.

Butter.

Buy the best you can find and afford. Look for a high butterfat content; the U.S. standard minimum is 80 percent fat. The better American and European butters are 84 to 87 percent fat. Ideally the butter is from cows raised on grass. Unfortunately, many of the local, small-batch butters I find from grass farmers are a little gamey. Irish Gold is a great supermarket butter. Kate's Homemade Butter, Vermont Butter and Cheese Creamery, and Straus Family Creamery make wonderful small batch American butters. Cultured butter is made by allowing a little natural lactic bacteria to ripen the cream. It's tangy and delicious. In every dish except biscuits and hollandaise I use unsalted butter.

Olive Oil.

Buy cold-pressed extra-virgin olive oil. Unfortunately, even that standard includes many lousy oils. Superior olive oils have low rancidity, but you can't read that on the label. Worse, many olive oils are illegally thinned with lesser nut and vegetable oils. Until the olive oil business devises a superior standard, you'll have to taste a lot of oils to learn what's nice and what's not, and rely on the better labels, such as Frantoia. On the labels of better oils you will find a batch number and best-by date, and all the olives will have come from a single farm.

Vinegars.

I love vinegar and every kind: red wine and white, Champagne, cider, balsamic, sherry, rice wine, ume plum. I recommend them all. A little extra money for better vinegar will reward you twice over. First, it won't bury the good oil you've bought; and second, the flavor—not the inherent sharpness, but the base character of the salty Japanese plum or the raw apple cider—will enhance your dish when chosen properly.

Herbs.

I use only fresh herbs, never dried, though homegrown and dried herbs taste better than commercial ones, which are often irradiated, stale, or both. I even prefer fresh bay leaves, although they are quite piney and best used sparingly.

Juice.

In my teens and twenties, I was a low-fat vegan and vegetarian with an awful juice habit. I was also moody and plump. Both the depression and the pudge vanished when I replaced juice with fat and protein. After that, I was an annoying, hard-core single woman who frowned on juice, and especially on the mothers whose children drank it. Too much juice is certainly not good for children—it's bad for metabolism and teeth— but now I've softened a bit. If the main drinks in your house are not sweet—milk, water, kombucha, coconut water—there's room for a little juice. Gently pasteurized ciders and other fruit juices from local farms enjoy a spot in our fridge, as does raw orange juice from the corner deli, especially in the winter. We drink juice, use it in salad dressings, and braise savory things in it. Today I crusade against pasteurized orange juice. Commercial orange juice is stored for many months, after which its juiciness is gone. It tastes like stale sugar water, with no flavor, so they add a proprietary orange juice "perfume" to make it seem juicy again. I won't even cook with it; you're just cooking down scented sugar water. For small recipes I buy Valencia oranges and squeeze them.

Unrefined Sea Salt.

Only unrefined sea salt contains dozens of nutritious trace minerals. When salt is refined—which may include heating, grinding, bleaching, and rearranging in flakes or other shapes—precious trace minerals in ocean water are lost and what's left is straight sodium chloride. Unrefined salt, by contrast, contains about 84 percent sodium chloride. The rest is magnesium, calcium, potassium, iodine, and other minerals and trace elements essential to every human function, from digestion to adrenal function to blood pressure. Don't buy plain "sea salt." Look for "hand harvested," "unrefined," and "traditional." Unrefined sea salt may be white, off-white, gray, or pinkish and slightly moist. Salts I like are Maldon, Celtic, and Jacobsen.

Baking Ingredients.

I recommend unbleached, American-milled King Arthur flours. The white whole wheat flour is milled from hard white spring wheat rather than the traditional red. It's a whole grain with a lighter texture and flavor than most whole wheat flours. I buy Bob's Red Mill baking powder, which is free of aluminum, and Bob's Red Mill baking soda, which is simply bicarbonate of soda.

Cocoa Powder and Chocolate.

Cheap cocoa is often bitter. Not Pernigotti, which has a rich, smooth flavor and 20 percent fat, more than other powders. It is so good my children drink "plain"—that is, unsweetened—chocolate milk. For baking and chocolate drinks, I buy eating chocolate. All my recipes are made with bars containing a minimum of 70% cocoa content. Pralus and Mast Brothers make superior chocolate. Lindt is a respectable supermarket brand.

Vanilla.

I'm happy to spend good money on vanilla. Some of that good money goes to Singing Dog Vanilla for organic and fair-trade extract and beans.

Sugar.

The white stuff is the one industrial food I cannot give up entirely. I love honey and maple syrup, but some things (like lemon curd) taste better with bright white sugar, and the other sweeteners leave me cold. Stevia tastes chemical. The agave "nectar" sold as a traditional and native sweetener is in fact neither. It's not made from the sap of the agave plant (aguamiel), but from a starch in the root bulb called inulin, which is then broken down by enzymes, or "hydrolyzed," into fructose. The glycemic index and glycemic load of agave nectar are similar to that of fructose. (Mexicans do make syrup by boiling aguamiel, but most Americans are not buying that.)

Instead of using phony sweeteners, I'd rather cook with Grade B maple syrup (the flavor is richer than in Grade A); raw honey (deep, diverse flavors, plus propolis, pollen, and enzymes); or the best sugar I can find, and ration my sweets. I eat few desserts and eat them not too sweet. Organic whole cane sugar (made by evaporating whole sugarcane juice) is my favorite sugar for desserts. It adds a lovely touch of caramel, which suits certain dishes, such as ice cream and fruit crisp. It's whole; whatever B vitamins and minerals sugarcane contains (and they are few) is all in there. Rapunzel is a good brand.

Molasses is what's left when sugarcane or sugar beets are processed to make refined sugar. Most brown sugar is nothing more than refined white sugar with molasses added back. You get a similar effect with whole cane sugar. For gingerbread, straight unsulfured blackstrap molasses—from the third boiling of sugarcane—delivers the characteristic dark, spicy thing.

THE SHOPPING LIST

An eclectic, personal, and incomplete shopping list for your consideration.

Local Food
For national listings of local food and an online catalog of many other real foods (such as chocolate), try Local Harvest.
www.LocalHarvest.org

Farm Shares
Also known as Community Supported Agriculture
You pay in advance for a farm share and get a weekly selection of local food all season. Farm shares include produce, flowers, meat, dairy, poultry, honey, and eggs.
www.nal.usda.gov/afsic/csa

Biodynamic Farms and Foods
Biodynamic famers follow the teachings of Rudolf Steiner. Biodynamic farms apply certain composts and minerals; use on-farm nutrients, such as animal manure; and follow astronomical planting schedules, among other techniques. Many grape growers and winemakers are using these methods.
www.Biodynamics.com

Citrus
Alas, there are no orange groves near New York City. Citrus is one of the regional foods I try to buy from smaller, ecological producers.

La Vigne Organics grows biodynamic and organic citrus in San Diego County, California, including unusual fruits such as minneolas, blood oranges, kumquats, and persimmons.
www.LaVigneFruits.com

South Tex Organics grows organic grapefruit, oranges, and Meyer lemons.
www.STxOrganics.com

Grass-Fed and Pastured Meat, Dairy, Poultry, Eggs, & Game

Jo Robinson, author of *Pasture Perfect,* provides excellent information on the definitions and benefits of grass-fed meat, dairy, eggs, poultry, and game. Her directory of farms is vast.
www.EatWild.com

The American Pastured Poultry Producer's Association knows the farmers you'll need.
www.APPPA.org

Backyard Chickens

Bug control! Chores for children! Pleasant company! Free pastured eggs! Well, almost free, after you pay for the chicken house and the feed. Chickens are great backyard animals. They like the front yard, too. Make sure they have plenty of grass to scratch in, a dry place for a dust bath, and lots of shade. If you don't have a bushes or a hedgerow, give them a tent.
www.BackyardChickens.com
www.BackyardPoultryMag.com

Butchers
Fleisher's Grass-Fed & Organic Meats

Joshua Applestone ditched his vegan ways and took up his grandfather's work as a master butcher. Order the meat, buy the cookbook, or take butchery classes. Find Fleisher's in Brooklyn and Kingston, New York.
www.Fleishers.com

Dickson's Farmstand Meats

Beef, lamb, pork, goat, and poultry from local farms raised the right way and butchered with care. The beef master stock is superb.
www.DicksonsFarmstand.com

Milk, Cream, Cheese, & Butter
Campaign for Real Milk

A Campaign for Real Milk describes raw-milk laws in each state and will lead you to buying clubs and cow shares for raw milk, butter, cream, yogurt, and other real dairy.
www.RealMilk.com

Organic Pastures Dairy Company

Organic Pastures Dairy Company sells organic, grass-fed raw milk, cheese, butter, and other dairy products in California. It's also the unofficial headquarters of the raw milk crusade.
www.OrganicPastures.com

Murray's Cheese

Murray's Cheese—my husband's shop—sells and ships American and European small-production, raw-milk, grass-fed milk, and farmstead cheeses. (Farmstead cheeses are made with the milk of the farm's herd.) Murray's also sells cured meats, fine chocolates, delicious olive oils, and various addictive items, like Spanish Marcona almonds. *The Murray's Cheese Handbook* makes a great gift.
www.MurraysCheese.com

White Cow Dairy

Superlative and original dairy foods made from the milk of a grass-fed family herd. Hard to find outside of Buffalo—but worth a trip to the farmers' market and his new shop if you're there. Or try Murray's Cheese.
www.WhiteCowDairy.com

Wild Fish & Seafood
Vital Choice

Alaskan salmon is wild. The state banned fish farming, so wild salmon and other fish are abundant in Alaska's clean, cold waters. The best fish is "frozen at sea" and shipped vacuum-packed. I used to list several excellent purveyors of clean, wild fish, but in practice I always go back to Vital Choice for salmon and roe, spot prawns, halibut, and sable fish, a silky, codlike fish I adore. So now it stands alone—on my shopping list, anyway.
www.VitalChoice.com

Fish Oil & Cod Liver Oil

Cod liver oil is valuable because it contains fat-soluble vitamins A and D along with omega-3 fats. All cod liver oil is refined to some degree, which reduces vitamin content. Most manufactures add synthetic vitamins back, but the brands below use only natural vitamin A and D. Some are flavored with mint, cinnamon, or citrus. For omega-3 fats, try wild salmon oil capsules from Vital Choice.

Dr. Ron Schmid, www.DrRons.com
Green Pastures, www.GreenPasture.org

American Nuts, Corn, Wheat, Rice, & Beans
Holmquist Hazelnut Orchards
On book tour in Seattle, I discovered Holmquist Hazelnut Orchards, a family business in Washington's Nooksack River Valley. It grows Duchilly hazelnuts, which are more delicious than any I've ever tasted. They're fresh, oval, and sweet.
www.Holmquisthazelnuts.com

Cayuga Pure Organics
Grows, mills, and sells modern and heirloom grains, beans, and flours in New York state.
www.CPOrganics.com

Anson Mills
Sells certified-organic whole heirloom seed corn, wheat, and Carolina gold rice grown on American farms in Georgia, Virginia, the Carolinas, and elsewhere. Grits and biscuit flour are cold-milled to preserve flavor and nutrients. Carolina gold and white rice is buffered and milled with traditional colonial methods. Anson Mills recommends soaking grits with potash or baking soda, the traditional Native American method of making grains more nutritious and digestible.
www.AnsonMills.com

Various Traditional Foods
Join the Weston A. Price Foundation to get its newsletter, *Wise Traditions*. The excellent classified section has ads for local grass-fed meat, poultry, eggs, and dairy and other traditional foods such as coconut oil and salmon roe.
www.WestonAPrice.org

The Grain and Salt Society sells traditional foods including unrefined sea salt, traditional fats, wild salmon, organic dark chocolate, and fermented foods.
www.CelticSeaSalt.com

Jacobsen Salt Co. harvests a delicious, pure salt from Oregon waters using traditional methods.
www.JacobsenSalt.com

Tropical Traditions sells unrefined, virgin coconut oil and a rich coconut cream from small organic farms in the Philippines.
www.TropicalTraditions.com

Acknowledgments

I'm grateful to Jennifer Unter, my agent and my friend, who has guided another book from under a bushel, perhaps into the light. I deeply appreciate Martha Wilkie, who made the whole project run smoothly with charm and wit and is a fine cook. My editor, Kathy Belden, has, for a third time, wisely and gently shepherded a heartfelt, raggedy manuscript into printable condition. At home, where the heart is, I thank Julian, Rose, and Jacob for their unrivaled company. Mother and children know that the meal is not complete unless Daddy sits at the head of the table. Rob, I thank you from my heart of hearts for the life we relish.

Emily Duff and Michele Pulaski taught me many recipes and how to cook them. They are women of great intelligence and high spirits, so all our times together are fun. In the 1980s, Emily helped to shape TriBeCa as a culinary spot. She worked at Greenmarkets for culinary-minded farmers like Frank Wilklow and Ray Bradley. She rides her bike to local markets, plays in a rock band, and writes about home cooking at Family2Table. Michele is a self-taught cook, the founder of DiSh catering in Frenchtown, New Jersey, and a veteran of twentysome restaurants, including Murray's Cheese Bar in New York City. Michele planned her New Year's Eve wedding feast of twenty-five courses in thirty days.

Index

Note: Italic page numbers refer to illustrations. Phrases in capitals are recipes.

A Note on the Author

Nina Planck grew up picking beans and tomatoes on a pioneering ecological farm in Virginia. In 1999, while writing speeches for the U.S. ambassador to Britain, she founded London Farmers' Markets, the first American-style farmers' markets in London. Local press dubbed her "The American" and "The Green Queen," and *ES Magazine* put her on its Top 100 list of Londoners. In New York City, Nina was the executive director of more than fifty Greenmarkets. She lives in New York City and Stockton, New Jersey, with cheesemonger Rob Kaufelt and their three children. www.NinaPlanck.com and www.LFM.org.uk.